THE
JEWISH
MYSTIQUE

THE
JEWISH
MYSTIQUE

by Ernest van den Haag

STEIN AND DAY/*Publishers*/New York

ACKNOWLEDGMENTS

I am greatly indebted to the work of J. Coleman, N. Weyl, L. Rosten, A. L. Sachar, S. Baron, N. Glazer, and many other writers, including S. Freud and, above all, the authors of the Old and New Testaments. Without them, this book could not have been written.

E. v. d. H.

Contents

Preface

I PROPOSE to write about Jews without hostility or apologetics, and with affection and seriousness, although my temperament makes me unable to resist occasional irony.

I hope to be accurate. But I should deceive myself were I to believe that accuracy in detail, and veracity about matters as a whole, are enough. For too many centuries the Jews have been used as a Rorschach blot by Gentiles, who attribute to them sometimes the most, and more often the least, desired traits of their own personalities. And for too many centuries the Jews have incorporated the image of themselves created by others and added it to their self-image. Under these circumstances any description will displease many who miss their favorite vices, virtues, and characteristics—or find those they prefer to ignore.

If this *causerie* be anywhere near as engaging as its subject, I shall have exceeded my most arrogant ambitions; if it be only half as ambiguous, I shall have done better than I feared. However, I shall be satisfied if it be recognized that I wrote *sine ira et studio*, and with apprehension.

E. V. D. H.

1

Are Jews Smarter Than Other People?

ASKED to make a list of the men who have most dominated the thinking of the modern world, many educated people would name Freud, Einstein, Marx, and Darwin. Of these four, only Darwin was not Jewish. In a world where Jews are only a tiny percentage of the population, what is the secret of the disproportionate importance the Jews have had in the history of Western culture? Are they, as both their friends and enemies seem to suspect, smarter than other people?

The ability to perceive new situations as new, and to find effective ways to meet them—the ability, further, to manipulate abstract concepts so as to discover principles and construct appropriate theories to connect them—this ability, as measured by I.Q. tests, is largely inherited. It can be trained. But what is trained is what has been inherited. (The success of training depends on motivation, too.) It is hard to distinguish the effect of training from the effect of inheritance, but not impossible; and the I.Q. test is far from a perfect measure. Still, when we find that genetically identical twins reared in different environments have nearly identical

13

scores, while brothers or sisters reared in the same environment display greater I.Q. score differences, the conclusion that inheritance plays a major role is inescapable. And the average I.Q.'s of Jewish children are consistently higher than those of non-Jewish children.

Of course this does not mean that there are no stupid Jews or intelligent Gentiles. One meets plenty of both. It simply means that, all other things being equal, the chances of a Jewish child's being intelligent are somewhat—we don't know exactly how much—higher than the chances of a non-Jewish child. Is this the manner in which they were "chosen" by God?

Well, one doesn't know how much God had to do with it. But the rabbis certainly did.

Among the Jews, literally for millennia, the brightest had the best chances to marry and produce children, and their children had the best chance to survive infancy. In contrast, in the Western world at least, the brightest non-Jews had the least chance to have children throughout the Middle Ages. (Outside the Western world, intelligence has been neither much of an advantage nor a hindrance in bringing children into the world and having them survive.)

Why did the most intelligent non-Jews, for nearly a thousand years, have the least chance in the Western world to produce offspring who would inherit their intelligence? Throughout the Middle Ages, the ecclesiastical career promised the greatest, fastest—indeed, nearly the only—advancement possible for those sons of the lowly born who were endowed with enough talent and intelligence to rise above the subservient position in which most peasants found themselves. The church offered the only career in which intellectual ability was rewarded, regardless of the origin of its bearer. No wonder the priesthood attracted the most ambitious, talented, and intelligent sons of the lower estates, and the most intellectual ones from the other estates.

But the priesthood exacted a price: celibacy. Which meant that the most intelligent portion of the population did not have offspring; their genes were siphoned off, generation after generation, into the church, and not returned to the world's, or even the church's, genetic supply. The result was a reduction of the average intelligence level of the non-Jewish Western population to a level considerably below that which would have been achieved otherwise.

The church's demand for ecclesiastical celibacy was based on at least three things. First, there was the general hostility of the church to sex. While the weakness of ordinary mortals might make it better to marry than to burn, priests were expected to have greater ability to resist temptation.

Secondly, a celibate priest would not be tempted to accumulate riches and power for children he does not have (at least he would be less tempted); he would love all Christians as a father without favoring his own offspring.

Finally, all medieval Christians believed in the salvation of their individual souls and the resurrection of their bodies. Such a specific belief in one's own individual immortality made it unnecessary to attempt to secure an immortality of sorts by producing and shaping one's own children. Yet Christians who were not priests were not quite willing to pin all their hopes on the promise of resurrection: faith was strong but not that strong. But priests, professional Christians as it were, were expected to set an example;

15

they had to renounce immortality through offspring in favor of individual salvation—with the consequent unforeseen, unintended, and unfortunate result that the intellectual elite had no offspring.

Celibacy was not always strictly enforced. And some priests or monks might not have wanted to have children anyway. But even when all possible qualifications are taken into account, there is little doubt that the rule of celibacy reduced the average intelligence of the non-Jewish Western populations. Consider how many outstanding scholars (let alone those who made minor contributions) descended from married Protestant ministers or Jewish rabbis. Had they, too, been childless, the contributions of their proverbially numerous offspring would have been lost. The magnitude of the contributions of the non-Catholic clergy's actual offspring suggests the size of the loss society suffered because of the celibacy of the Catholic clergy in the many centuries during which Catholicism dominated the Western world.

Today, while the abolition of clerical celibacy is being discussed in Catholic circles, celibacy no longer does much genetic damage. There are many opportunities other than the priesthood available to people who want to go beyond the status achieved by their parents. The church no longer offers the only nor the best chance for advancement of an intelligent but poor boy in most places, and there are many intellectual careers outside the church. It may be surmised that children of low-income families who enter the priesthood now do so more often because of an unworldly vocation; worldly ambition even among the poor can be achieved more easily in other ways—ways which do not preclude offspring.

Among the Jews, the most intelligent were encouraged to have the most children: they became rabbis, who could afford—indeed were expected—to have lots of children. Rabbinical study even more than the priesthood among Gentiles attracted the brightest and most ambitious Jews. After all, the rabbi was the leader of the Jewish community in every sense of the word.

Abstract philosophical issues, questions of ritual, commercial disputes, marital problems—whatever matters were of importance—ultimately were decided by interpretation of precedents, and the rabbi's interpretation was the most authoritative. Hence the rabbis had the prestige, the power, and the prerogatives of leaders. Unlike their Christian colleagues, they did not have the competition of secular leaders, kings, and judges. The rabbi was the religious *and* the secular leader of the Jewish community. Thus, boys who today might become judges, lawyers, political leaders, physicians, teachers, scholars—all became rabbis.*

Unlike priests, rabbis were enjoined to marry and have children. In turn, rich men were enjoined to give their daughters in marriage to rabbinical scholars, the Jewish aristocracy. Both these injunctions were followed in practice; they were in the spirit that informed Judaism as a whole throughout the Middle Ages. The results were:

1) The most intelligent, ambitious, and intellectually inclined Jews became rabbis.

2) Rabbinical students and rabbis married earlier than other Jews—they were regarded as more eligible.

---

* Today's American rabbi, of course, has been shorn of this leadership; he has become—except for the highly orthodox—merely the religious leader of a congregation, which often is itself barely religious.

3) Rabbinical students were able to marry the daughters of the most successful Jews and generally had the widest choice. These choices were not based on personal attraction but on the reputed health and wealth of the prospective bride. Some correlation is likely between intelligence and success; the daughters of rich men must often —by no means always—have inherited intelligence as well as money.

4) Rabbis, able to support more children more easily than other Jews, had more children.

5) More of their children survived because many rabbis had some knowledge of medicine; further, as leaders, they could give their families more protection than other Jews. (The selective process was compounded when high marriage taxes were imposed on Jews in Central Europe, as was often done into the nineteenth century. These taxes made marriage easier for the well-to-do who could better afford them.)

Above all, rabbis sedulously followed the Talmudic injunction to be fruitful. Altogether, if Jews had deliberately decided to breed children so as to maximize genetic intelligence, they could not have done much better. Of course, they had no such conscious purpose—any more than the Catholic rule of celibacy was intended to reduce the average intelligence of Christians. These results were incidental to other avowed and conscious purposes. Nevertheless they have profoundly affected the history of the Jews, and indeed, of the world.

"Intelligence" actually consists of a variety of mental abilities: e.g., verbal ability (retention and relations of words); reasoning (conceptualization, interpretation, and inference); mathematical ability (manipulation of numbers); space conceptualization (ability to relate, visualize, and manipulate sizes and shapes). Many other mental abilities are also involved. Some are hard to measure. The various tests give a specific weight to each tested ability and call "intelligence" some sort of compound—which in the nature of the matter is rather arbitrary and has a purely theoretical existence: only the components exist and operate separately.

Certainly one person may excel in, say, mathematics, but have little literary intelligence. Another may be a mathematical moron but extremely clever verbally. Yet both may test as equally "intelligent" if, say, the higher mathematical aptitude of the first offsets his lower verbal score and the higher verbal score of the second offsets his poor mathematical score. Whether or not this occurs depends on the relative weights assigned to the different aptitudes by the particular tests. Yet the better tests succeed fairly well in identifying and grading something that deserves the label "ability to reason abstractly or conceptually." And this ability is highly important in a number of careers. Therefore these tests have significant predictive value.

Though these tests are useful, one must be wary of their limitations, and above all, one must not conclude that they define fully an individual's abilities, or measure adequately such human virtues as creativity, imagination, emotional predispositions, and ultimately character. (Other tests may help in evaluating such elements of "personality.")

For what it is worth, Jewish children generally do better than other groups on I.Q. tests. And the more weight that is given to verbal and reasoning abilities, the better they do. They do better on practically all scores except space conceptualization, where Chinese children are usually superior. These differences among ethnic groups are specifically ethnic—they remain, regardless of social class, status, or schooling.

"Ethnic" should not be confused, however, with "genetic." We do not know how much of the greater intelligence found, on the average, among Jews as an ethnic group is inherited through the genes. In all likelihood the result is, in some unknown proportion, owed to cultural as well as genetic factors.

That cultural factors play a major role (and may, in time, have influenced genetic ones, since culture may cause the preferential selection of the possessors of the most highly valued traits for marriage and breeding) is clear to anyone even slightly familiar with the enormous emphasis on learning, intellectuality, articulateness, and argument—even argumentativeness—that is characteristic of Jews.

The emphasis on intellect within the home, the family, and the community is transmitted to children at an extremely early age and greatly intensifies their motivation toward the achievement of educational goals. According to the values of the community, this is the way to gain the approval of one's elders, to be respected and, in the end, to be successful.

This certainly has been the case of the Ashkenazim, the Jewish group that lived in Western and Eastern Europe. That group, surrounded by a Christian world, not only preserved its religion but lived—partly voluntarily and partly of necessity—a separate life in which the Jewish ideas, the Jewish character, and the Jewish intellect were formed. While the majority of Christians lived on farms in the countryside, the majority of Jews, neither serfs nor allowed to own land, lived in the city. Thus Jews have long been accustomed to urban values, which are relatively new to most Gentiles.

Another Jewish group, the Sephardim, lived mainly along the North African perimeter, surrounded by an Islamic world.* They were assimilated in all but religion. Even where not assimilated, the Sephardic Jews did not pursue separate Jewish ideals; in particular, their respect for and interest in scholarship did not compare to that of the Ashkenazim, but rather to that of the surrounding Moslems. This difference may have been caused by the comparatively fewer disabilities imposed on Jews by the Moslems, who usually were more tolerant of Jews than were medieval Christians. (How things have changed!)

The results of this difference can be seen easily, not only in Israel, where the Sephardim sometimes feel treated like a minority, but also in the United States. In both countries the scholastic achievement of Sephardic children is far below that of the Ashkenazim. In Israel the Sephardic children come from a deprived background, from families with little education, income, and status. But recent tests in the United States have shown that this is not likely to be the cause of their low educational achievement. The United States' tests compared two groups of Jewish children —one Sephardic and the other Ashkenazic—attending separate private schools. Both groups came from middle-class

---

* The Sephardic Jews who lived in the Iberian peninsula were culturally ahead of the African Sephardim.

parents, were American born of American-born mothers, spoke English at home, and lived in the same middle-class neighborhood. Yet the Sephardic children scored, on the average, 17 points less on the I.Q. tests than the Ashkenazic —about the same difference as in Israel.

Oddly, the difference is about the same, on the average, as that between white and black children in the United States. One may speculate that the explanation is similar, particularly since recent research * suggests that the differences between whites and blacks are ethnic far more than they are related to schooling, or even to segregation, or class.

The only possible explanation for the different test results among Jewish groups—since differential opportunities or economic deprivations were excluded—is a difference in cultural ideals and emphases, internalized as a difference in motivation. (Genetic differences are unlikely, since both groups are Jewish, although they have lived apart for thousands of years.) Unlike the Ashkenazim, the Sephardim have never focused on educational achievement. This result suggests that the difference in Jewish-Gentile achievement and intelligence, too, may be largely due to a difference in values cultivated at home, whatever additional role genetic factors may play.

The higher average Jewish intelligence and scholarly motivation lead to considerable scholarly achievement. Sixty-seven American scientists received Nobel Prizes between 1901 and 1965; eighteen of these—27 per cent—

* E.g., the "Coleman Report," *Equality of Educational Opportunity* (U.S. Department of Health, Education and Welfare, 1966) prepared by James Coleman under the 1964 Civil Rights Act and published by the U.S. Government.

were Jewish. Jews constitute about 3 per cent of the population. Thus they produced about nine times as many Nobel Laureates in science as statistically could be expected. The overrepresentation would be reduced if Jewish Nobel Prize winners in science were taken as a proportion not of the Jewish population but of Jewish scientists. However, this would be useful only to the extent to which Jewish overrepresentation among scientists depends on factors other than intelligence and motivation. I don't think it does.

Thirty per cent of all high school students plan to go to college—but 75 per cent of all Jewish high school students have these plans (both figures increase year by year). And their plans are carried out: Jews, as a proportion of the population, are overrepresented by about 260 per cent in the college population and by 365 per cent in the elite institutions.

Jewish students succeed well in college, as measured by future earnings—higher on the average than those of Gentile college graduates. They also enter professions more often: they are overrepresented by 231 per cent in medicine, within medicine by 308 per cent within the specialties, and among these by 478 per cent in psychiatry, and 299 per cent in dentistry. Outside medicine, Jews are overrepresented by 265 per cent in law, by 283 per cent in mathematics—but only by 70 per cent in architecture (which is explainable in terms of their no more than average talent for space conceptualization) and 9 per cent in engineering. The low overrepresentation in engineering might be explained by past employment discrimination in industry and by the comprehensiveness of the term "engineer," which includes skilled workers as well as professionals. Despite the fact that relatively few Jews are engineers, they are 110 per cent overrepresented in invention.

Jewish overrepresentation is partly a matter of motivation. Lewis M. Terman, who followed the careers of gifted children in California, found that of those who were Jewish, 57 per cent entered professions, while only 44 per cent of the gifted Gentile children did. Yet only 15 per cent of the Jewish parents were professionals, while 35 per cent of the Gentile ones were: a clear indication that Jewishness reinforced motivation toward professional careers independently of the professional or nonprofessional parental status. Terman also found that about twice as many gifted children were Jewish as would be expected on the basis of Jewish representation in the California population. This, once more, must be attributed to genetic and motivational factors in unknown proportions.

An increase in Jewish representation in the professions took place as soon as Jews became emancipated in the United States—as soon as purely religious careers lost their attractiveness for many, and barriers to college admission were lowered. Thus, in 1922, Jews were represented in the Phi Beta Kappa scholarly elite about in proportion to their representation in the population. But in 1962, the number of Jews in Phi Beta Kappa was 33 per cent above what could be expected on the basis of their representation in the total population.

It might be worth mentioning that although by no means all minorities display extraordinary gifts, the Jews are not the only minority that does. The Parsi, originally a Persian group, settled in India where they kept their religion and many cultural peculiarities. This group, too, has been disproportionately successful in business and in the professions. The fate and the environment of the Parsi, let alone their original cultural and religious customs and beliefs, are quite different from those of the Jews. Yet like the Jews they differ from the society in which they live, and feel, as Jews have, psychologically marginal to it.

It is possible, as some philosophers and sociologists have speculated, that this marginality contributes to the motivation and cultivation of achievement as an attempt to compensate and prove oneself. Yet it cannot be minority status alone that brings about this effect, for the motivation is more common than the supposed reaction to it. Thus minority status, however necessary, cannot be sufficient to bring about intellectual eminence.

2

Who Are the Jews and What Were They Chosen For?

THE STUBBORN, clumsy, almost absurd integrity of the Jews was no doubt one of the reasons why James Joyce in *Ulysses* made Leopold Bloom his Homeric hero: not a Greek, or an Irishman, but a Jew. Yet Bloom is not very "Jewish." Many emancipated Jews are not. This too is a frequent Jewish trait: a reaction to their ethnocentric past. Bloom does not seem religious; he is not very involved with other Jews, apart from his wife; he does not engage in any particularly Jewish activity. He is Jewish only in one thing: it does not occur to him *not* to be a Jew. To cease being a Jew, to become something else in religion or nationality, is inconceivable to him—though one does not know why.

No doubt, Bloom stands for humanity on its voyage of discovery. In one day he experiences the human career on earth and symbolizes the human, not the Jewish, predicament. But he is a Jew. Nobody is a Jew by accident. Joyce chose a Jew to stand for humanity. He makes him suffer indignities—self-inflicted in a way. But even when groveling obscenely, Bloom retains some sort of stubborn dignity. No, that is not the word. Humanity is better.

Where does it come from? Jews are human, we all are, but Jews are in a sense more human than any one else: they have witnessed and taken part in more of the human career, they have recorded more of it, shaped more of it, originated and developed more of it, above all, suffered more of it, than any other people. No other nation has witnessed so much, argued and bargained so much, and yet clung to its own inner core as much as the Jews have. They are the perennial fathers, accused, ritually murdered, yet always revived by or reincarnated in the sons who have violently slain them.

For over 2000 years now they have dazed, dazzled, and befuddled the world. They gave our civilization its pre-eminent religion—but refused to share it, suggesting that this Messiah was for the goyim only. A better one would come—but only for them—at a later time.* They have been waiting stubbornly since. A patient people; or are they?

They have given the world some more Messiahs while waiting. And they had a few spurious ones of their own. They gave us Karl Marx, who wanted to save the world by socialism; but Marx was anti-Semitic. He saw Jews as creatures of capitalism, and he hated them also for more personal reasons. They gave the world Sigmund Freud, but, in effect, refused to hire him at the University of Jerusalem.

Not only are Jews ambiguous about their own great men; they are ambiguous even about their own existence.

* Theologians would say correctly that the Jewish Messiah was expected to redeem the whole world. The popular idea here described disregards theology and expresses what people *felt*. Incidentally the Jews were concerned with prophecy, ethics, and the Law. Theology in the main is a Greek contribution to Christianity.

At times they deny that Jewishness is a religion, a race, a nationality, or even a culture—and nearly pretend that it is just something invented by anti-Semites. At other times they imply that non-Jews must be tolerated—God created them too, but why?—although not taken seriously.

Who, then, are the Jews—since, despite all arguments to the contrary, they do exist palpably enough to be killed by a Hitler? Negroes can be recognized by the color of their skin. Not so Jews—they are of all colors. Above all, Jews are ambivalent, almost coquettish. They will go to great lengths and give you numberless instances (though telling you in the same breath that " 'for instance' is no proof") to show that there is no Jewish physical type: German Jews look like Germans and French Jews like Frenchmen. Of course, Jews also say that they can recognize a Jew just by looking at him. The only thing they won't be is pinned down: experience has taught them that to be pinned down is dangerous.

Is there a Jewish mentality? character? spirit? Heaven forbid! some Jews will exclaim, insisting that Jews are just like other people only they call their church a synagogue (a Greek word) or schul (a German word). Other Jews—or sometimes the same ones in a different mood—will say that there *are* Jewish character traits—nice ones, of course. And they will explain what makes the Jews so Jewish. Which would be fine, except that just as sometimes they claim nothing for themselves and deny even that they exist as a group, at these times they claim everything: everybody outstanding is either Jewish or ought to be. As the mother of a good friend of mine used to say of anyone she regarded with favor: he *must* be Jewish.

Having lost their original geographic home, the Jews

clung to their spiritual home—their laws, customs, and beliefs—and to each other. They identified with one another through their common background; they distilled the essential identification into personality, intellect, and social life. Without an earthly location of their own, they clung to their heavenly destination, the God who chose them—a universal God, the only true God, and yet their God, by mutual choice.

Just as their God is universal, yet peculiarly theirs, so are many other values. The Jews have clung to and insisted on reason as a universal criterion applicable in all situations. Irrationality has been their enemy. So has tradition. Reason has been their weapon against the traditions, institutions, and superstitions * of the Gentile world—for all these served to exclude them. The Jews have been egalitarians—for inequality placed them in the inferior position. They have learned to identify with the oppressed, the humiliated, the suffering—for usually they have been among them.

And yet, no people is more traditional or clings more stubbornly to its customs; no people is more parochial and discriminatory in its feelings and attitudes than the Jewish people. The temper is dogmatic. So is the rationalism. Even Jewish liberals are dogmatically tolerant (and quite intolerant of those who are not, or who tolerate different things). How else could they have survived with their Jewish identity intact? It is this combination of dogmatic traditionalism about Jewish customs and utter traditionless rationalism about anything else, that made it possible for these people to survive as Jews, to reject the traditions that might absorb them, and to retain their own.

A paradox? Yes, perhaps, and essential to the Jewish

* A word I just invented and like.

character, which is an incarnation of the problem inherent in rationalism and dealt with by ambivalence—or, if it is to be avoided, by polarization. To admit that reason does not and cannot explain and, above all, replace the experience of the human career seems perilously near to abdicating and inviting unreason. To pretend that reason can do what it cannot do is to deceive oneself and to refuse to perceive what one cannot understand; it is to deny experience. Such presumptuousness might invite worse dogma than the mysticism risked by acknowledging the limits of reason. Thus the Jews, ferociously rational, reserved one corner of the universe to tradition: theirs.

All religions have attempted to avoid the horns of the rational-mystical dilemma. And all have reserved mystical corners to themselves while challenging others to defend their faith by reasoned argument. In this the Jews were no exception. But from the viewpoint of rational defense, they had some practical advantages. Their own original faith was in no need of defense: it was shared by their adversaries. The Jews just rejected certain developments of it: Christianity. These additions and changes were as hard—though no harder—to justify by reason as was the original faith; and they, too, were universally shared—but not quite; for the Jews rejected them. Defense against the Jews, the fathers who had repudiated their offspring, was imperative for Christianity. Subsequent centuries responded with anti-Semitism, which finally developed into the prevalently negative yet ambivalent Jewish mystique produced by the Gentiles.

As for the Jews, no other group's fate has been so affected by the mystique it created for itself, and by the effects of the mystique created by others. Jews (like the devil) became both ridiculous and powerful, contemptible and uncanny, superior and inferior, feared, despised, and sought-after. Despite their importance to Christianity, they became and remained nearly unknown to most Christians.

The question, What is a Jew? has puzzled Jews and Gentiles alike. The latter have sometimes found it easier to kill those called Jews than to define what makes them Jews. And the Jews all too often have been content to be defined by their enemies—as victims.

For Jean Paul Sartre, Jews do not exist: "It is not the Jewish character that provokes anti-Semitism," he says with perhaps more generosity than accuracy, "but rather anti-Semites who create the Jew." Sure; and Jews, when speaking to their enemies, seem to agree. Properly speaking, they say, there aren't any Jews. People like Hitler imagined them. (Unfortunately, Hitler killed real people.) Jewishness is not a religion, the argument continues, and never, but never, a race, or even a culture. These "enlightened" Jews find odd allies for this opinion among the rigidly orthodox Hassidic sect. To the Hassidim, who believe that Jewishness is at once a religion, a race, a people, and a culture, modern emancipated Jews do not exist as Jews at all (much as the Mormons call Christians who do not believe in the prophecy of Joseph Smith "Gentiles," strangers outside the fold).

The problem of definition is no easier for non-Jews. To some Nazis, Jesus was not really a Jew, but Roosevelt was. To others, Jesus was a Jew, wherefore Christianity was tainted and had to be abandoned. To some Jews, such as Sigmund Freud, Moses was not really a Jew (he was an

31

Egyptian), and the Mosaic religion (like all others) was no more than an anodyne and a collective neurosis. Karl Marx, as anti-Semitic as a storm trooper (and as vulgar when, for instance, he called his rival Lasalle a "nigger Jew"), defined Jewishness as a particular kind of nastiness, bound to disappear when capitalism does.

His followers in the Soviet Union agree and are not above helping the disappearance along by giving Jews a push into oblivion here and there. Stalin liked to do so physically. To be fair, his successors prefer to exterminate Jewish culture while sparing its bearers. They say to the Jews: if you only stop being Jewish, you can be one of us. The gambit is age-old and was refused steadfastly in the past. To be sure, unlike the Nazis, the Communists persecute Jews for religious and not for racial reasons—a distinction which must seem rather subtle to the victims.

Of course, Marx's enemies regarded him as a Jew, though his father, who was not religious and didn't care one way or the other, had converted to Lutheranism for convenience. Jewish Marxists abound, but so do Jewish anti-Marxists; many leading Bolshevists were of Jewish descent, but so are many of the leading anti-Communists in the United States and Russia. The Jewish Marxists who defined Jewishness as a religion, and thought themselves at last rid of it when they became atheists, just brought a grim smile to the lips of their enemies—they had become *Jewish* atheists. To be a Jew is clearly not just a matter of religion.

Repudiation of what they have given—even self-repudiation—seems a Jewish characteristic. Religion is one of the main instances. There is no people historically more concerned with religion than the Jews, who first made the

Bible out of their lives and then made their lives out of the Bible. Yet great numbers of the most famous men the Jews have given to the world either repudiated their own religion for another or repudiated all religion—though many of them continued to feel as Jews and all of them to be counted as Jews.

If Jewishness is not, or not entirely, a matter of religion, what is it then? Is it a feeling? I think the answer here is at least a partial "yes." More perhaps than anything else, a man's feeling that he is, like it or not, Jewish makes him a Jew. This feeling, even when ambiguous, even when unconscious, often makes others feel so, too—regardless of denial, conversion, or apostasy. The feeling justifies itself. Should it be so? I can only give a Jewish answer: why ask me? Is it so? On the whole, and instances to the contrary notwithstanding, yes.

The feeling cannot be willed. You can become a Catholic by conversion. But a Jew? Does anyone regard Marilyn Monroe or Elizabeth Taylor as Jewish? Did they care seriously? To be sure, they did rhetorically. But the will took the place of what was willed. They wanted to be Jewish (i.e., accepted by their husbands) and thought that made them Jewish. But Jews are born, not made.

Legalisms apart, a Jew is counted as one, regardless of baptism or atheism, if he comes from a Jewish family. (This is not true, however, in Israel, where to count as a Jew he must not have converted to Christianity. Jews are but a series of exceptions.) This was one part of the complicated truth which the Nazis grasped. (Enemies are often more clear-sighted than friends.) But in their own distorted way, the Nazis went on to say that a man was Jewish even if only one of his eight great-grandparents had been Jewish, and even if he was not considered Jewish by other Jews. The Nazis deemed him Jewish even if his family had been Christian for many generations. (If this seems odd, consider popular feelings about what percentage of "blood" makes one a Negro.) Distinctions and definitions can become absurd when pushed too far—which does not detract from their soundness on a common-sense level. And on that level, a Jew is a person of predominantly Jewish descent.

This is a social as distinguished from a racial or religious or cultural definition—for clearly, many people whose ancestors were religious Jews are themselves not. The South African tycoon Oppenheimer (DeBeers diamonds, Anglo-American Corp., etc.) is an Episcopalian. Einstein was not a believer although, like Freud, he regarded himself as Jewish. Marx, as we said, was Protestant. Clearly they are all Jews. And what about Barry Goldwater? But Sammy Davis, Jr., can't make it, no matter how much he would like to be a Jew. And Marilyn Monroe just married one; she would have liked to marry his background and religion as well, but couldn't do it. Neither Davis nor Marilyn Monroe could *feel* Jewish. But even if by some miracle they could, they would never be regarded as Jews by Jews.

The Jews are nonevangelical and rather discourage would-be converts. Disavowals notwithstanding, Judaism has essentially remained a tribal religion—even though the Jews invented the most evangelical of the non-tribal religions. When the Apostle Paul made a Jewish sect into a universal religion, he had given up hope for Jewish conversion. And once Christianity was preached to the Gentiles, chances for the conversion of the Jews were reduced to near zero. They would not join a religion that denied their chosenness.

It is often believed (particularly by their friends) that Jews share physical characteristics more with the inhabitants of the country in which they live than with Jews from other countries—German Jews seem more German than Jewish, Italian Jews more Italian than Jewish, Yemenite Jews more Arab than Jewish. But this is only partially true: true often enough to be believed generally, but not generally true. It would stand to reason, of course, owing to long residence and similar geographic, nutritional, and social environment, let alone intermarriage. Indeed, German Jews can be very Germanic (in the eyes of non-Germans) and Russian Jews very Russian (in the eyes of non-Russians).

But what stands to reason seldom works with Jews. Tests made in Israel show quite definitely that if one considers blood type frequency, or types of fingerprint whorls, Yemenite Jews, though separated from them for thousands of years, have more in common with German Jews than German Jews have with non-Jewish Germans, or Yemenite Jews with non-Jewish Yemenites. In short, the inherited characteristics of Jews—the genotype—seem quite well preserved, at least in these specific respects. How important this is for less easily measured, but more important characteristics such as psychic ones, which may be acquired more often than inherited, is hard to say. But to the extent that one can speak of a genotype, one can speak of a Jewish genotype, and one can say that in comparative terms, it is remarkably pure. It seems that Jews have, on

35

the whole, followed the Biblical injunction to keep to themselves and to shun intermarriage. Up to now.

Scattered among alien cultures as they have been now for over two thousand years, how are we to explain this remarkable homogeneity of the Jews? The answer is, in the first place, religion—religion as an all-pervasive norm of conduct and regulation of daily activity. And second, Jews kept their identity because they were not allowed to forget it. A hostile environment took care of that. In the past, their religion distinguished them and led to discrimination against them in the same fundamental way in which skin color today distinguishes Negroes; for his religion was regarded as part of a man's existence, character, status, and predicament the way skin color has been.

To the Jews religion quite strongly retained its literal meaning of *re-ligare,* to re-link. As constantly expounded, interpreted, and elaborated by the rabbis, the Jewish religion became The Law, organizing and regulating every detail of Jewish life in such a way as to keep Jews apart from any other group, strengthening their solidarity and continuing their existence as a sharply identifiable community. External pressures against this alien body, the unending Christian hostility to the Jews, who refused conversion, who lived in their midst but repudiated the essence of the faith which they had generated, merely hardened the institutional structure of the Jewish community.

Christian hostility caused untold suffering borne patiently by the Jews—there was little else they could do other than be converted—but above all, it led to their isolation from the non-Jewish world. Thus their identity was preserved with the help of those who worked to destroy it.

36

Without that hostility, they will survive in greater material comfort and security—but will they remain Jews now that they are no longer forced to be either Christians or Jews?

Although regarded as innovators and anti-traditionalists, the Jews are the most tradition-minded and conservative of all peoples. To be Jewish is to cling to a set of practices and rituals, sacred and profane, to a set of activities and institutions, religious and secular, to a set of attitudes more than to any elaborate beliefs. Above all, the Jews cling to the promise their God made them—even when they no longer believe in God. The promissory note is to be redeemed even after the maker has died—it is a lien on his wealth. Because of the promise, the Jews cleaved to their God. Because of cleaving to their God, they remained Jews. And to remain Jews, they had to do and omit all the things they did and omitted.

In a sense, the promise was fulfilled. They survived where others perished. And they survived as Jews. They even managed to compel the admiration and acceptance of the Gentile world, in which they now occupy leading positions in nearly any branch of activity. Had they not been traditionalists clinging to every law, they could not have remained Jews. And yet, had they not been innovators, unfettered by tradition, creating and utilizing new devices, they could not have survived, let alone achieved what they did achieve.

And innovators they were. There is no new industry, or science, no new movement in art or literature, no new theory in psychology or physics, no new movement in politics or religion in which Jews do not play a prominent part. One simple explanation is, of course, that a high proportion of Jews are intellectually gifted and highly educated. Intellectuals are by definition critical and innovative. Education usually renews tradition as much as it transmits it. However, the highly educated Jew is probably more ready for innovation, on the average, than the highly educated and equally gifted Gentile.

The Jew receives his education in a culture which, though it originated in great part in his own religious tradition, in its secular form is quite different from his own. And he receives it in schools that are dominated by these partly alien traditions, and attended mainly by non-Jewish pupils. He accepts consciously both the people and the traditions, and excels in the skills. But there may well remain a spirit of opposition, an ambivalence in the acceptance that implies a rejection at the same time. And that rejection may well take the form of innovation—for to innovate is always, if not to reject, psychologically at least to overcome, to discard the old.

Einstein was quite dissatisfied with the German Gymnasium he attended. There was little anti-Semitism at the time—at least he did not complain about it in his later autobiographical writings—and he had not come from a piously Jewish home. Nonetheless he found the Gymnasium's atmosphere uncongenial to his Jewish sensibility. Later, in Switzerland, he absorbed Newtonian physics. Whereupon he went beyond it, to show that Newton's physics applied only to a special case which Einstein's physics could include, but did transcend.

Freud studied and learned the neurology and psychology he was taught in Vienna, but was not content with it. He went to France to study the new ideas of Charcot and Bernstein and returned finally to explore wholly unexplored parts of the human psyche and to develop a revolutionary theory of personality.

One may find in the Jewish tradition itself an innovatory as well as a traditional spirit. It is a tradition oddly polarized and balanced between the absolute authority of the law and freedom of cumulative interpretation and adaptation; between the immense authority of the interpreting rabbi and the minimal institutional framework of that authority.

Few are the nations whose recorded history goes back so far and is so complete as that of the Jews; their written history starts with the creation of the world: Genesis. And it includes the wanderings, the battles, politics, family trees and family skeletons, social policies, economics, the successes and failures, and above all, the moral history of this people which believed itself chosen by God for a special destiny, and which—because of that belief—suffered a remarkable fate.

What were they chosen for? Certainly the Jews *have* been "chosen," if only for suffering and for survival as an identifiable and continuous group. The Egypt of the Pharaohs which kept them in bondage—where is it now? Mummified in museums, remembered by matzo balls. (Egypt never seems to have been lucky with the Jews—though it is too early still to decide by what dish to remember Nasser.) Babylon vanished; so did the Assyrians. Imperial Rome conquered Jerusalem and vanished—as did the glory that was Greece. Tribes such as the Moabites or the Philistines are remembered now only because they fought the Jews, because they became part of Jewish history.

The languages of these civilizations are, at best, preserved only in academic spirits; but Hebrew is still chanted and spoken. It is today once more the language of a country, of the state of Israel—a state which already twice defeated the surrounding Arab tribes, including, this time, Egypt for good measure. Conquered, their capital laid waste, their temple burned, banned from their land, dispersed through history and scattered over the world without king or country, everywhere persecuted, declared enemies of mankind and murderers of God—the Jews remain. And remain Jews. They still believe themselves the Chosen People,* even though, contemplating their long history, one may well ask, "Chosen for what?"

As I am writing, the Jews merrily celebrate their 5730th year. For most of these 5730 years, they lived in circumstances so adverse as to defy the imagination. They survived; most of their tormentors did not. Still, even with the patience of Job, they may well begin to suspect that they were chosen for suffering. Nor has their suffering ended. Nazism is gone and Hitler is dead. But so are six million Jews.

Myths and the mystique that compounds them can become part of the reality they are meant to suggest. Indeed some of the more sanguine philosophers of Madison Avenue claim that the images they fashion become part of the product they advertise. They certainly try to fuse—or con-

---

* Secularized Jews and Jewish intellectuals seldom admit as much, but they act as if they feel even more chosen than those who do.

fuse—the image and its object, and occasionally they succeed.

Sometimes such a fusion, off Madison Avenue, is quite unavoidable. The images created by poets and historians, for instance, are naturally and spontaneously related to their object. The poet's image of the world necessarily affects the world to which it holds up the mirror: readers will experience the world, and react to it, through the literary image, and they may even act to make the world conform to the poet's image.

Historians, on the other hand, are convinced that their image of the past is quite like the past. Luckily for them, their image is the only means through which we can experience the past. And although history may be "the bunk" as Henry Ford is supposed to have said, historians must and do make sense of it; they must give it significance—or else they could not write anything intelligible: they would have to list an endless series of facts without rhyme or reason, without distinguishing the "important" from the "unimportant." The world always has been full of facts. To write about it is to select, to decide what is important, which means to have decided what it is important to, and for—or to give history meaning. In our own life we select, each of us, analogously what is significant. Our individual selection largely depends on our culture, which is characterized by its selections.

It is the Jews who have given the essential meaning to the last two thousand years of Western history. They started by attempting to give meaning to their own life, to create a mystique for their own use. It had a great deal in common with the mystique of other peoples, but it was distinctive, if not unique, in several respects that remained part of the Jewish religion. Ultimately, a Jewish interpretation of human destiny came to be almost universally accepted—only to be repudiated by the Jews, who were unwilling to lose their group identity by participating as individuals in a larger group; they clung to their group identity, thereby confronting hardships, hostility, and even hatred. Their choice cost them an immense price paid over the past two thousand years. But it was a bargain nonetheless, for it helped unite the Jews and keep them a cohesive, identifiable group. One needn't be a Jew to understand why Jews value what has cost them so much.

Voltaire once pointed out that Christian historians seem to suggest "that everything in the world had been done on behalf of the Jewish people . . . if God gave the Babylonians authority over Asia, He did so to punish the Jews; if God sent the Romans, He did so to punish [the Jews] once more. . . ." He went on to ask: "Why should the world be made to rotate around the insignificant pimple of Jewry?"

Voltaire did not try to answer his own obviously rhetorical question. Yet it might be asked seriously. For the history of the Jews is still more widely read and known than any other, and it is incomparably the most influential of the histories of the Western world. For centuries it has been a source of inspiration: the history of the Jews became the Bible. It has been used to make the world intelligible, to justify the universe and its Creator, not only to the Jews before and after Christ, but to Christianity and Islam as well. The Bible is not only the best-selling book of all time, but also the most widely read.

42

Most peoples see themselves as the center of the universe. But why did the rest of humanity finally share the Jewish version of world history? Why did they all believe the world rotated around the Jews? Why did Jewish history become the prototype for the history of the world? If the Jews are as "insignificant" as the nonbeliever Voltaire suggests, why did this numerically tiny and powerless people loom so large in Western history?

To believers, the answer is plain. The Jews were important to God, so they must be important to all who believe in Him. But many nonbelievers, too, such as Hitler, thought the Jews important and powerful beyond their numbers. Why are they believed to be important not only by their friends, but even more so by all their enemies? Their existence itself seems uncanny, as does their relationship to the rest of the world. How did they arouse—and survive—so much hostility? Will they survive emancipation? Now that they have their own territorial state once more, will they survive as a cultural and spiritual entity? The question sounds paradoxical. But Jews are but a series of paradoxes.

The Jews are and were at various times in history the most despised and the most sought-after and needed people. They were constantly expelled from Christian countries only to be reinvited, constantly robbed only to become rich again, curbed and oppressed only to be suspected of secretly running the world and, of course, of causing all that goes wrong with it. Much of this was done in the name of one of their own.

For though they did not recognize Jesus as the Redeemer, He certainly was a Jew, as were His apostles. The

Jews suffered through many centuries for refusing to accept their own kin as mankind's Redeemer. But to this people, often regarded as overly materialistic or rationalistic, the price never seemed too high. They have refused to this day the acceptance which would have ended their sufferings, for to accept Him would be to end their existence as an identifiable group, as the Chosen People. No wonder that a legend should have grown about a people so ubiquitous and well known yet so mysterious and full of contradictions, so shrouded in mystery yet bathed in the glare of historical records better known than those of any other people.

3

Is There a Jewish Character?

THE JEWS have invented more ideas, have made the world more intelligible, for a longer span and for more people, than any other group. They have done this directly and indirectly, always unintentionally, and certainly not in concert, but nevertheless comprehensively. The lives of us all in the West (as well as in Russia) and even of vast areas in the rest of the world have been strongly influenced, if not altogether shaped, by a view of human fate which is essentially Jewish in cast and origin. Jewish influence continues, not only through our common religious heritage, which clearly bears the marks of its Jewish origin, but also through the constant addition of new, nonreligious ideas produced by Jewish scientists and scholars. To be sure, the Jewish view of the human career on earth—of its genesis, purpose, rewards, and pitfalls—has had its own career. Any creed that persists so long must be expected to change and develop. More remarkable, however, is the continuity of the core of the Jewish conception of human fate for so long a time.

Certainly Jewish groups, factions, movements, or persons do not all hold the same ideas; nonetheless the persistence of some common beliefs leading to common practices and attitudes has been sufficient to leave a strong residue in the Jewish character. Attitudes are transmitted from generation to generation, and they are intensified when the external conditions which originally supported them remain unchanged. They become part of the character of the group.

At first glance, the idea of a "Jewish character" may seem absurd or, worse, an anti-Semitic stereotype. Individual Jewish characters certainly differ. So do characteristics. And often Jews stand at opposite poles of almost any conceivable range of beliefs, practices, or positions. Some Jews are very poor, others are very rich. (Most are somewhere in between.) Certainly this influences their characters. Some are ruthlessly ambitious for material success —they want above all to "make it" wherever "the action is"—others are gentle and other-worldly. Some are sensualists, others puritans. Some purvey the worst vulgarities of our culture in soap operas, musical comedies, TV, and general *Kitsch,* others are among the finest and most sensitive literary and social critics we have. Some (e.g., Norman Podhoretz's *Making It*) combine intellectual gifts with success-oriented ambition, and perhaps with a renunciation of any identity other than that of succeeding—not an uncommon traumatic effect of sudden emancipation. Some * are Communists, others are on the extreme right. (Most are

---

* Most reviewers identified the subject of this autobiographical book with the author. They then reviewed the author adversely for candidly presenting his success ambition. Yet the book presents only part of the author's personality. What matters is how well he projected it, not the critics horror of the ambition, which the critic repudiates in himself and does not like in the book.

in the "liberal" middle.) Some are criminals, others judges. (The Jewish ambiguity toward the law and conscience is illustrated in the career of Judge Leibowitz of New York State. One of the most successful criminal lawyers the country has ever known, he defended notoriously vicious mobsters and killers. Elevated to the bench, he has become equally famous for his severity in sentencing the criminals he used to defend.) The Rosenbergs, atomic spies, were Jewish. So is Judge Kaufman, who sentenced them to death.

Do Jews have things in common then, other than religion or descent, to transcend the many political, cultural, moral, psychological, social, economic, etc., differences that divide them and sometimes set one against the other?

I believe so. It is not, to be sure, any one thing. Rather there is a complicated network of overlapping and crisscrossing similarities and traits which occur and recur with greater than chance frequency among Jews. It is the resemblance that members of the same family may bear, even if some are nuns and others whores; some rich, others poor; some illiterate, others academicians; some atheists, others priests; some beautiful, some ugly. The similiarity is not in what is done or thought, but in the way that it is done, thought, felt, believed, or expressed. And even this kind of family resemblance is a matter of frequency: it is not equally pronounced in all members of the group. The Jews obviously are not homogeneous. Yet the group is identifiable genetically, culturally, and psychologically by the relatively higher frequency of certain traits. Contradictory surface manifestations are produced by these traits, but the traits, more often than not, are the common source of these reactions.

There are three common elements deeply inherent in

Judaism (the religion) and Jewishness (the character of the tribe and nation formed by the religion). The first of these elements is messianism; the second, intellectualism; the third, a moralistic-legalistic outlook.

From these common elements many seemingly contradictory ideas, actions, and styles can be derived. This includes the socialism, communism, atheism of some Jews and the conservatism and religious dogmatism of others; the civil disobedience of some and the insistence on lawful conduct of others; the intolerance of some—e.g., Communists, or sometimes, anti-Communists—and the tolerance of others; the puritanism of the rabbis, and Norman Mailer's frenzied attempts to defy it and to free himself from it, or Philip Roth's no less talented, or, at times, less obscene or frantic attempts to do so.

Roth, however, uses obscenity where it belongs: there is obscenity in his art, whereas there is art (often) in Mailer's obscenity. Two different ways—Roth's more sublimated than Mailer's—of defying one's past? It seems likely. Mailer usually writes primitively idealized fantasies of himself—disguised as an Irishman—whereas Roth deals more directly and realistically with his past, trying to acknowledge and reabsorb what Mailer tries to deny by his disguise.

Unlike the other peoples of antiquity, the Jews not only believed in a paradise lost—the reign of Saturn to the Gentiles—but also in a paradise to be regained. This divine promise, to be redeemed by the Messiah—which Christianity elaborated, stressed and extended beyond the chosen people—underwent many modifications among both religious and nonreligious Jews, but it never was written off. Among the religious, it was felt that redemption depended on the Jews keeping their side of the bargain. Strict observance and interpretation of the Law became necessary because the Messiah would not come until all the Jews were virtuous and deserved paradise.

Judaism and Jewishness coalesced into an unending series of rules of conduct that identified Jews, made them cohere, set them apart, and made them suffer yet persist. For the promise was going to be redeemed. God was not going to go back on the bargain. And since the virtue of all the Jews was necessary to the descent of the Messiah from Heaven, it became the duty of every Jew to urge all other Jews to adhere to the Law and to their God. On this basis the intense community of the Jews was separated from all other peoples throughout their long history.

Emancipated Jews who, under the impact of the enlightenment, of industrialization, and of science, left their religion, secularized the idea of redemption as they did other Jewish values. Rationalism itself contains a promise of salvation: the idea of progress, the idea that by means of appropriate reforms and careful thought we ourselves can create the paradise that the Messiah was to establish. The idea that paradise can be achieved, whether by upholding or by overthrowing the law, is common to the religious Jew as well as to the anti-religious Jewish radical; it is an essentially Jewish idea.

To be sure, non-Jews can be, and are, Utopians, too. They are, knowingly or not, influenced by their Christian heritage, which contains the salvationist idea derived from Judaism. But the far greater frequency with which Jews dedicate themselves to messianic schemes is a direct result of the secularization of their traditional religious beliefs, which strengthen not only faith in salvation but also the conviction that salvation requires knowledge of some ineluctable law. Marxist theory, for instance, with its notions of historical necessity, can easily take the place of talmudic scholarship. And often does.

As for justice, the Jews are the only people who have entered into a legal contract with their God—the covenant He made with Noah and with Abraham. Jews pray to their God, but also bargain and demand that He live up to His side of the agreement. And it is the law and the constant reinterpretation of it, the belief in justice and the practice of the intellectual legal version thereof, that has kept the Jews Jewish.

At first glance, it may seem unreasonable to derive either the messianic Utopianism which in religious or secular form has been a characteristic of Jews, or the moral drive for social justice and equality, from the prophetic Judaism in which they first appeared. Why should ideas pronounced 2500 years ago in a minor kingdom in the Middle East now influence Jews scattered in various places under the most diverse conditions? They would not, but for circumstances and institutions that kept these ideas alive.

When, after three unsuccessful rebellions, the emperor Hadrian banned the surviving Jews from their territory, many had already left. The more reasonable and moderate Jews, unable to forestall the rebellions of the Zealots and all too able to see the hopelessness of their attempt to defeat the Romans, had settled in various parts of the world. Some did not resist the influence of their new environment, but most followed the rabbinical injunction to keep apart, to live according to the Law which prohibited marriage with Gentiles and prevented more than casual relations with them.

According to the historian Josephus, as Jerusalem seemed about to fall to Vespasian's legions (actually, it fell only later to those of Vespasian's son, Titus), Rabbi Jochanaan ben Zakkai was sneaked out of the besieged city, hidden in a coffin. Rabbi Jochanaan was a leading Pharisee, that is, a moderate conservative; the Sadducees were the pro-hellenistic reform elements; and the Zealots were zealots in both politics and religious fundamentalism. (It is remarkable that these three elements—reform, conservative, and fundamentalist—can be seen once more in modern Judaism. But then circumstances have become similar: a secular, non-Jewish world beckons again.)

The leaders of the anti-Roman rebellion, themselves divided by factional strife, were Zealots, and the Pharisees had to lie low. Nonetheless, Rabbi Jochanaan surrendered to Vespasian in the name of the then actually powerless Pharisees, and in exchange obtained from him permission to open an academy of Hebraic studies. Vespasian was aware of the rabbi's powerlessness, but he thought the formal surrender politically useful in Rome. It officially ended the war and conveniently classified the further fighting, at least temporarily, as a police action.

The rabbi's institute, which flourished first in Japneh and later in Babylon, created a tradition that never wholly disappeared from Jewish life. It recreated Jewish identity and made it independent of territory, temple, and political organization: as invisible, and as strong and demanding, as the Jewish God. It achieved the transfer of legal and religious authority from God and His priests and prophets to the divine Law and its scholarly interpreters—the rabbis. These learned interpreters proceeded almost immediately to do three things that made possible the bond which has held the Jews together, cemented them into communities, and the communities, however scattered, into a nation. A nation without territory, government, or sovereignty—but still a nation. Owing to this tradition, cultivated by the rabbis, Jews continued to feel the yoke, the task, the moral mission of being Jews—of preserving themselves as such, and to the surprise, scorn, and at times hatred of the rest of the world, of refusing to become anything else.

This mission has been internalized deeply and pervasively, even by Jews who deny its *raison d'être* and regard talk of a chosen people and religion itself as so much superstition. Jews may call themselves humanists, or atheists, socialists, or communists; they may indifferently or passionately repudiate any reason whatsoever for remaining Jews; they may even dislike Jewishness and feel it—to use an apt metaphor—as a cross they have to bear. They may deny its existence in scientific terms. But rarely do they refuse to carry it, though they continually grumble and threaten to throw it off, and deny that they are getting anywhere, and haggle with God, the world, and their friends about the compensations they are to get. They will not be cheated out of the promised redemption, though the expectation is vague and ritualistic in some, altogether unconscious in others. They won't give up being Jewish even when they consciously try to, when they change names, intermarry, and do everything they can to deny Jewishness. Yet they remain aware of it, and though repudiating it, they cling to it; they may repress it, but do act it out symptomatically. Their awareness of their Jewishness is shared by others simply because the denial is always ambivalent. Unconscious or not, at least some part of every Jew does not want to give up its Jewishness.

The first of the three vital steps taken by the long line of rabbis who laid down the law to the Jews was to codify this Law—the Old Testament. They decided what was, and what was not, Holy Writ. A body of history and prophecy was created, identical for all, which henceforth constituted the Jewish religion. The binding power of that codification stood the test of centuries. Indeed, the Jews, together in Jerusalem before the Diaspora, were divided into more sects and factions bitterly fighting each other than they were most of the time after their dispersal.

Secondly, the rabbis codified the ritual of worship, which became identical for all Jews.

Thirdly, and of immense importance, beyond worship the rabbis codified conduct which was to be inextricably linked to religion and to Jewishness. To be a Jew meant to follow numerous rules of conduct about eating, marrying, intercourse, children, education—about almost every detail of life. These rules of conduct served, together with ritual and belief, to set Jews apart from non-Jews, to keep them apart, and to keep them together. Not only were Jews warned against marrying non-Jews, they were prevented from even eating with them.

These three things separated the Jews from the rest of the world and provided a common center of belief and practice around which they could unify. The rabbis thus replaced the destroyed temple and its sacrifices of cattle only to impose a life of continuous self-sacrifice and ritual on the Jews. For to keep the minute rules and the comprehensive regulations was a heavy burden. Jews, for good measure, were enjoined to bear it joyfully.

Individual practices, of course, required adaptation when circumstances changed. These were provided in continuous interpretations—in response to problems as they arose—given by a long line of rabbis. Interpretations were in turn reinterpreted and re-reinterpreted *ad infinitum* in every Jewish community.

And the community was just that. The synagogue was its center; the rabbi represented the community and decided what should be done with regard to the Gentile environment; he was the judge in religious and civil matters; often he was the physician; always he acted as "human relations counselor." He was the final authority for every problem, practical or theoretical, that arose in the community. All this by virtue of his dedication to and knowledge of the Law.

This authority, derived from his study of the Law, contributed to the immense respect the Jews developed for learning. Together the Jewish communities did constitute a nation even though not sovereign or ruling over territory. Their internal affairs were left to them to regulate according to their Law (at least until emancipation) by their host nations. And their regulation had a distinct national style.

Such a long period of following the precepts laid down in the series of commentaries that shaped Jewish life and governed behavior and attitudes toward the outside world could not but be internalized. As it was transmitted from generation to generation, it left profound traces in individuals formed in these communities and resulted in characteristics which form a character—a character which remains in the modern secularized Jew who has abandoned the precept of which it is the precipitate.

None of the Jewish traits, however characteristic, is uniquely Jewish. Whether one considers attitudes toward the family, or money, or education, there are non-Jewish individuals who have identical attitudes and Jews who do not have "Jewish" attitudes. Nor is the totality of such traits in their relationship to each other—the character— altogether peculiar to Jews. There are non-Jewish individuals whose total character is within the range of "Jewish" character types; their circumstances may have been such as to produce a character-type of the Jewish sort. And there are Jews with "un-Jewish" characters. Further, there is not one Jewish character, nor even one prototype, but a range of character types.

This range overlaps with some others, in some aspects and segments—e.g., the Italian or Spanish character—but it does not fully coincide with any other. This entitles us to speak of those within it as "Jewish" character types. And secondly, the Jewish character types, those within the Jewish range—though also occurring within other groups, and not necessarily extending to all members of the Jewish group—occur within the Jewish group more frequently than outside. This, too, entitles us to speak of a specifically "Jewish" character.

Thus:

1) The Jewish character includes a range of character types with individual variations, even though

2) not all Jews have Jewish characters, and

3) not all non-Jews lack Jewish characters, for,

4) more Jews conform to one of the Jewish character types than do non-Jews.

That much to show that there can be, indeed there must be a Jewish character, and to show what it means if a character is attributed to a group. I have yet to describe at least some traits of that character, which I will do throughout the following chapters. Let us see how history took a hand in forming them.

4

To Suffer Is to Survive—and Vice Versa

BY MEANS of rude and painful shocks, history taught the Jews one important lesson. The didactic method was not progressive, but it was effective; and learning the lesson was vital: only the better students survived.

The lesson started in Canaan and goes back to the many Jewish uprisings against the Roman conquerors, each ending in the heroic but ineluctable defeat of the rebels. In 70 A.D., defeat, by Vespasian's son Titus, discredited the Zealots who—over the dead bodies of Pharisees and Sadducees—had led the Jews into the next-to-final useless heroics. The defeat this time cost the destruction of the temple and the loss of what little independence the Jews had retained. Heroic gestures fell altogether into disrepute sixty years later when the collapse of Bar Kochba's guerrillas ended in the plowing up of the soil on which Jewish Jerusalem had stood, and the elimination of most of its population: killed, sold into slavery, or dispersed.

The subsequent life in the Diaspora as a small and powerless minority, universally hated and precariously tolerated by overwhelmingly stronger majorities, intensified the impact of a lesson first grasped and taught by Rabbi

Jochanaan, at Jabneh, and demonstrated over and over again by history: unless there is a chance of winning, it is worse than useless—it is self-defeating—to react violently to whatever unbearable conditions an adversary imposes; it is suicidal to allow oneself to be provoked to violent reactions against an enemy, however insufferable his exactions, unless he can be defeated. This lesson, incessantly reinforced by the experiences of millennia, was finally internalized; it became a permanent part of "the Jewish character." Individual Jews who failed to absorb it sufficiently focused hostility on themselves; they were likely to die a violent death before their time—more likely than others, who were better adapted to the circumstances in which all Jews had to live. Jewish communities that failed to heed the lesson disappeared.

The rabbis intellectualized and justified this lesson of history. They taught that deliverance must come from God. We are being punished for our sins; in the end God will keep the Covenant, but meanwhile we must be patient; we must not try to force His hand, we must not fight enemies when our defeat is certain, we must dedicate ourselves to the meticulous fulfillment of His law; and in addition to being His Chosen People, we can remain spiritually superior to our more powerful enemies. We can cultivate our intellects—for this, no permission is needed. And we can excel in the activities permitted us.

This is exactly what the Jews did.

When the enemy is overwhelmingly stronger, when any violent resistance must end in defeat and bring even greater and more extended suffering, the only chance of survival lies in developing a vast tolerance for unjust burdens, in learning to suffer without striking back. By clinging to this lesson, the Jews adapted themselves to reality and managed to survive individually and collectively. A small powerless group surrounded by hostile and powerful masses can hope to survive only by never defying them, by not responding to challenges, by suffering mutely, by making itself as inconspicuous as possible and as useful as possible to the powers that be.

Thus, at infinite cost to their self-esteem, the Jews managed to be tolerated physically, if in no other way. For they were never accepted.

They not only survived, but stubbornly survived as Jews. Being universally rejected, they never rejected themselves. Unlike other minorities who faced equally hopeless odds against insurrection, the Jews were not demoralized by the humiliations heaped on them and by their own passivity. They perceived the Gentile image of them, and, as have other minorities, absorbed some of it. Yet, unlike Negroes in the United States, the Jews managed to keep alive a prideful endogenous self-image from which they could draw sustenance and which helped them to survive psychically intact; throughout history the Jews were able to keep and to sharpen their identity—and to make major contributions to civilization as soon as they were given an opportunity to do so.

Unlike Negroes, the Jews could fall back on their past history, recorded in the Bible and universally respected and accepted. Those who survived in the Diaspora never were enslaved. They were denied the rights others had, and deprived. But, with all that, they were permitted to live in their own style. And again unlike Negroes, in the dispersal Jews were able to form homogeneous communities, bound together by their own history, language, literature, and religion, and governed in internal affairs by their own political, social, and religious leaders.

Negroes lacked all of these intangible but immensely important advantages. They did not share a common language, religion, history, or culture; they had no literature, no record of their own past, no laws, no leaders, and no community. Tribes did have at least some of these common bonds; but enslavement destroyed the tribal units, and the Negroes kept on a plantation could communicate with each other only in English. Even their religion, their self-image, and their ambitions were those handed to them by their owners. They are in the difficult situation of not being accepted by the only society they know, of wishing to reject it in retaliation, and of having no society of their own, no culture, no usable past to turn to. (University studies and institutes cannot manufacture a history and a culture.) And the conditions which surrounded their life in America from the beginning hindered the development of those values, ambitions, and aptitudes which would have procured them a reasonable place in American society. In contrast the Jews were conditioned by their past to develop just those values, skills, ambitions, and talents which turned out to be most conductive to success in the industrial, business, and scholarly groups which dominate America.

Negroes did not feel that a code of conduct prescribed by their religion would lead to redemption, independently of the wishes of the white majority. They did not feel that their sufferings were a chastisement imposed by a Father who had been disobeyed and that ultimate redemption would depend on their studying and obeying His law. Unlike Jews, they tended to feel that their fate depended on outside secular forces—on the behavior of the white majority. Thus, they are led to pull or push that majority into helping them, and into repairing the damage done—which further weakens their own initiative and independence.

To be sure, the Jewish self-image could never be wholly independent of the image the Gentiles had of Jews. Nobody escapes unscathed from the role into which the world has cast him. The Gentile image was reflected and partly incorporated into the Jewish character. Even the defenses against it are, after all, reactions to it.

One trait of the Jewish character clearly represents this identification with the aggressor: the various forms of Jewish anti-Semitism. In its most virulent form, this is exemplified by the—very few—Jews who, hiding their Jewish descent, actually joined anti-Semitic groups (or, without hiding their Jewish descent, financed such groups). One such man some years ago committed suicide after a *New York Times* reporter exposed him. (The cruel and senseless action of the reporter was not so much anti-Semitic as it was inhuman. Perhaps the reporter himself was repudiating his own—realistically controlled—unconscious anti-Semitic wish when he vindictively exposed a harmlessly deranged unhappy person.)

Most Jews who have incorporated some of the anti-Semitic attitudes of their environment find far more rational ways of expressing it. The lively and sometimes excessive self-criticism of the Jews may well be interpreted as an expression of the originally external aggression that became part of the Jewish character—although the Bible clearly demonstrates that this self-criticism preceded the Diaspora. The Jewish superego seems always to have been

extraordinarily powerful—as one might expect in so patri-
archical a society—whether it found expression in prophets
or in later social critics. Nonetheless, some highly destructive Jewish self-criticism bears the earmarks of identification with the aggressor. Some is expressed in jokes—a
harmless way of discharging aggression.

Not the dialect jokes that people circulate about Jews.
These tell us something about the people who made them
up, not about the Jews. Nor the sometimes very funny ones
that nightclub comedians (mostly Jewish themselves) invent, and which often gain enormous popularity before
they die out. We've all heard too many of them, and
besides, they are not characteristic of the jokes the Jewish
people tell about themselves to themselves. Jokes perhaps
not as funny as the professional ones, but which nevertheless come closer to expressing the underlying philosophy
of Jews.

Sholom Aleichem, one of the most famous of all writers
in Yiddish, defined hope as "a liar." He said, "April First
is a joke that is repeated three hundred and sixty-five times
a year," and, "Life is a drama for the wise, a game for the
fool, a comedy for the rich, and a tragedy for the poor."

"When does a poor Jew eat chicken?" goes a riddle in
the folklore. "When he's sick. Or else when the chicken is."

You can almost hear the sigh of acceptance with which
these jokes were met when first heard in the wretched *Stetls*
of Eastern Europe. This is the humor of the deprecating
shrug, jokes which rarely make you laugh with the deep
roar of pleasure that characterizes much non-Jewish humor.
At best, these jokes make you smile for a moment, and that
smile is rueful. Jews say they make jokes in order not to cry.

Their jokes about the harshness of the lives they led for so many centuries are intended to take the sting out of suffering—as though suffering itself were funny. It is almost as if they go out of their way to make jokes about themselves, in order to anticipate the pain the world has in store for them, and by this anticipation, blunt its impact.

"How are things?" one Jew asks another.

"Good!"

"I'm glad to hear it. I heard you were in trouble."

"No, it's always good. In the summer, I'm good and hot. In winter, I'm good and cold. When it rains, I catch a good cold, and my wife's nagging about money makes me good and mad. And finally, I'm good and tired of it all."

Or take the—not necessarily funny—story of August Belmont and the assembly. The famous banker, who was born poor and Jewish though he died rich and Episcopalian, was a strenuous social climber at the beginning of his career. When he heard that his name was not on the select list of guests to be invited to some particularly glittering assembly, he demanded to see the committee who drew up the list. As the story goes, the powerful banker then threatened each man on the committee with financial ruin unless the decision was reversed and an invitation issued to Belmont. He got it.

"That's what power will do," said a non-Jewish friend of mine to whom I told this story. "It serves that stupid committee right, the snobbish bastards." And he chuckled over the discomfort of the committee.

I told the same story to a Jewish friend of mine. "What happened?" he asked. "Did Belmont go to the ball and find that no one else had shown up?" And he sighed for the fate of Jews, for whom, he felt, every triumph is only a penultimate build-up, preparing the way for the crashing defeat of the punch line. Unlike my Gentile friend, he did not feel the story was "right" if it ended with the triumph of a Jew. He therefore went on to invent a deprecatory ending of his own; inevitably, he felt, the world would supply it if he didn't. But since he supplied it first, the damage was inflicted by himself, and therefore, minimized.

This last also illustrates another facet of Jewish humor: it rarely is overtly aggressive toward non-Jews. Yet "playing a joke on someone," who becomes "the butt" of the joke, is clearly a form of aggression and the basis of much humor; the aggression is permissible precisely because it is not serious. But in most Jewish humor, the joke is on the teller; he turns aggression against himself; he feels he cannot afford to attack the actual target even in fun. There may be retaliation, and he is weak. He prefers to identify with the feared non-Jewish environment and attack himself, as though to say: you can't hurt me anymore than I can—I have already done it.

Two Polish Jews who kept taverns (one of the occupations Jews were allowed) were discussing business.

"When I sell a man drinks on credit," said the first, "I make him pay double."

"Not me," said the second. "I charge only half of what I get when they pay cash."

"That's silly. Why do you do that?"

"Because that way, when he doesn't pay me, I only lose half as much."

When it allows itself to hit back at the outside world, Jewish humor tends to do it obliquely, and the anger vented must be paid for: often the price is self-deprecation. But not always.

"Everything that is rotten in the world," said the anti-Semite to the Jew, "is the fault of the Jews."

"That's true," said the Jew with great conviction. "You're absolutely right. The Jews and the people who eat bananas."

"Why people who eat bananas?"

"Why Jews?"

Evidently the Jewish character is changing in Israel, but until the recent Israeli-Arab wars, the Jewish avoidance of violence and aggression was universally acknowledged and ridiculed by others—and by Jews who were embarrassed by what they could not help. A Jew was conscripted into the army, even though he pleaded that he was a pacifist. At the height of battle, the sergeant rallied the troops.

"All right men," he cried. "We're going to charge with our bayonets, and win this battle in man-to-man fighting!"

"Please, Sergeant," said the Jew. "Could you just point out my man to me, and maybe I can come to a quiet understanding with him?"

Cultural inhibition against aggression has been internalized among the Jews; it was functional. If they responded with violence to Gentile provocation, Jews jeopardized the Jewish community and achieved nothing else. From a religious viewpoint sufferings in the Diaspora, and the dispersion itself, were imposed by God for the sinfulness of the Jews. Tolerating suffering thus becomes a pious act following God's will. To rebel against this divine chastisement would be a sin. So the Jews almost glorified masochism, telling themselves that since God loved them the most, he punished them the most. Just as material success was one of the signs to the Calvinist that God's grace was being showered on him, so the Jew came to feel that suffering was his seal and symbol of being chosen.

However, the failure of Jews to discharge their resentment against others in acts, or even in symbolic actions such as jokes, does not indicate lack of resentment. Shakespeare's Shylock was in this respect a correct—and fearful —intuition. People so long mistreated will seek revenge when they can. The modern Jewish jokester will make self-aggressive jokes and use them to legitimize the aggressive jokes he now also dares to make against the Gentile world. The Marx Brothers caricatured Jews—and thus allowed themselves to caricature the Gentile world as well. And Chaplin presented an affectionate caricature of the powerless Jewish immigrant—and a far from affectionate caricature of the Gentile world into which he had migrated.

Internalized anti-Semitism of course can lead to more, and worse, than jokes. *The Armed Prophet,* who having achieved power uses it ruthlessly, may well have learned something from his original enemies. And the hostility of various Jewish groups toward each other—rationalized on religious, political, cultural, or economic grounds, even on ethnic ones—may owe something to the internalized enemy too.

Nevertheless, the endogenous Jewish self-image, carefully cultivated in a lifelong process of education, remained strong enough to vouchsafe survival and self-respect. The essence of it was that God had chosen the Jews for a special destiny which required their suffering and absolute fidelity to the laws He had given. These laws, which constituted Jewishness, had to be interpreted and lived continuously by the community and by its rabbis. Faithful to His part of the bargain, God finally would send the Messiah and deliver the Jews when they had suffered enough.

This lived tradition and the self-image it fostered enabled the Jews to respond with secret contempt to the open hatred and to the overt contempt of the Gentiles. They suffered wounds. They were psychologically no more invulnerable than physically; but they survived and continued to believe that God had chosen them. Suffering did not shake, but rather confirmed their faith.

As soon as the Jews were emancipated from oppression, their psychological wounds started to hurt. As their faith weakened with their externally induced suffering, they often became victims of the injuries suffered in the past. It is no accident that Jews invented psychoanalysis, which deals with and sometimes heals psychological wounds by explaining the present in terms of an internalized past which has to be reexperienced in more favorable conditions. To quote an untypically guarded statement by Sigmund Freud: "Nor is it perhaps entirely a matter of chance that the first advocate of psychoanalysis was a Jew." Psychoanalysis has become the best comfort available, and also the least absurd, for those who lost their faith but not the need for it.

The price was high. But their adaptation, at this high price, bought the survival of the Jews. Survival—survival as Jews—for millennia was their first priority. For that they suffered; for that they bore burdens no slave could be lashed or bribed into bearing; for that they underwent toil which no pleasure or pain addressed to the senses would lead one to undergo. For that, and because of that, they survived. Honor and pride were luxuries they could not afford. They had to follow the wisdom ascribed to Solomon: "Better a live dog, than a dead lion"—provided they could be live Jewish dogs. For Jewishness was the one thing they refused to give up—to give it up was to give up life now *and* hereafter.

Passivity was not enough. The Jews needed and managed to get some protection through the law, and through the ecclesiastical and worldly powers that fashioned it, by making themselves useful to these powers. To be sure, the protection was tenuous enough. The Jews were easily and often sacrificed for the sake of something more important to their protectors. In good times the princes and the ecclesiastical dignitaries found Jewish financial and other skills useful enough to protect the unpopular group. But whenever their subjects, aroused by excessive misery, by misfortune, or by misgovernment, needed to discharge their anger and frustration, the same princes would use the Jews to divert popular ire away from themselves. It was an uncomfortable and dangerous life for the Jews; but no other was possible if they wanted to remain Jews. And even as scapegoats, they were useful enough to be tolerated if only to be available for the sacrifice. To be Jewish was to be compelled to be what the Gentile world regarded as vile, to suffer infinite humiliation, to be bereft of dignity, honor, beauty, or any aspiration but that of clinging to one's Jewish life.

Some of the members of the community that survived by acknowledging its weakness and bending with the wind suffered considerable distortion of their character. Possibly even the community as a whole was at least temporarily affected. For instance, the adaptive idea: do not provoke the enemy ever, you can only lose; do not defy or oppose, you will only make things worse; to suffer in silence is your best chance to survive—this correct adaptive idea can be pushed (as all correct ideas can be) to ridiculous and incongruous lengths. Jews well recognize as much in a revealing joke: Two Jews were being put against the wall by a Nazi firing squad. One began loudly calling for a blindfold to cover his eyes. "Ssh," said the other, "don't get them mad."

Whether the number of victims slaughtered would have been reduced had the Jews defied and resisted the Nazis more often, had they "cooperated" less, is a moot question. I cannot see the point of telling a man who lost his family to ruthless enemies that his family might have saved itself had it acted more cunningly, or more courageously. The vast majority of Jews could not fathom the fate prepared for them. The madly systematic cruelty of the Nazis took place on so unheard-of a scale as to deprive it of all credibility. It was inconceivable to reasonable people that the government of a major, civilized nation could decide irrationally yet systematically to slaughter millions of harmless, innocent, and useful people for the sake of a set of silly and patently incredible folk tales. Realists, and Jews had learned to be realists, tended to discount as unreasonable, or as fantasy, what indeed was fantastic—a sadistic fantasy bereft of any but psychological rationale—but was, this time, to become actuality.

One can hardly blame them. Their realism was based on past experience with anti-Semitism. In that light, the Nazis must have seemed unreal. History had not prepared the Jews for systematic genocide. They had met cruel enemies, enraged mobs, wicked governments, but not systematic, comprehensive, efficient, and coordinated efforts to achieve total extinction. Historical experience seemed to indicate that the best way to deal with the storm was to lie low and wait until it passed. Some lives would be lost, and even some communities. Many would lose their property. All would suffer. But the best way to minimize loss and suffering was to be passive; resistance would gain nothing and infuriate the enemy further. The storm would pass, most would survive, and Jewish life would continue. It was hard to realize that Hitler was not a storm that would wear itself out, but a man dedicated to the preparation of a holocaust combining *furor teutonicus* and the vaunted efficiency of the industrial age. By the time they realized what was happening to them—that the storm was not blowing itself out, but was blowing them into gas ovens—it was far too late to organize effective resistance, though valiant acts of desperate resistance, particularly in close-knit communities, still could and did occur.

I do not know whether different Jewish strategies would have made a great difference. But the strategy adopted was generated by what had happened to them previously. That there was a qualitatively different element in the situation —that the Nazis were something totally new—was easy to see after the event. It was not before.

5

Why Anti-Semitism?

Jews "cause" both anti-Semitism and pro-Semitism; without them we would have neither, since both are reactions to Jews. The Jews are the cause of anti-Semitism in the sense—no more, no less—in which marriage is the cause of divorce. No divorce without marriage. No anti-Semitism without Jews. But to end in divorce, there must be specific elements in one or both partners of the marriage, or in their relationship to each other, or to other persons, that lead to divorce. So with the relationship of Jews to their environment. The Jews are necessary to anti-Semitism—but not sufficient. Why is the relationship what it is? Why is it so often hostile?

An anti-Semite is hostile to Jews because of some characteristics which he dislikes and which he thinks Jews have exclusively, or in greater measure than non-Jews. Whether they do or do not have these traits (and whether one regards them as valuable or vile), there must be something in the Jews, or in their situation, that invites the attribution of these characteristics to them rather than to bicyclists; in addition, there must be something in the

71

character of anti-Semites that makes it possible, or necessary, for them to associate Jews with disliked characteristics, or to dislike characteristics which Jews have because it is they who have them.

The characteristics attributed to "witches" burned in the seventeenth century, though sometimes accepted by the "witches" themselves, were the products of the fantasy of their persecutors. But there also was something in the personalities of those singled out as witches, or in their relationship to the world, which invited the attribution; just as there was something in the personalities of the witch-hunters which convinced them of the need to fear and hunt witches. The only thing we can be sure of is that the "something" was not that the women actually were "witches." Similarly we can be sure that what arouses anti-Semitism is not what Jews actually are; it is, as it were, the negative part of their mystique.

To say that the victim had some characteristics that led to his victimization, is not to excuse, or justify, those who victimized him any more than it excuses, or justifies, a murderer to point out what characteristics of the victim caused the murderer to single him out and kill him. It means, however, that there was something about the victim —actual or, if the murderer is insane or misled, only believed—that led the murderer to select him. It may be a "good" or "bad" characteristic or a neutral one: political prominence, virginity, promiscuity, beauty, or wealth, may happen to attract the murderer, and may lead him to kill the victim.

There certainly are traits, actual or putative, that distinguish Jews. If one loves or hates a person or group, one has oneself the ability to do so, and one's object has the ability to arouse and focus these feelings—whether because of actual or of putative qualities. What Gentiles see in seeing Jews is likely to be a compound of the Gentile mystique about Jews and of reality—the latter being shaped by both the Gentile and the Jewish mystique.

PRE-CHRISTIAN ANTI-SEMITISM

Fundamental to either view or feeling, though seldom explicit and conscious, is hostility to the Jewish belief in one God, a belief to which anti-Semites very reluctantly converted and which they never ceased to resist. Anti-Semitism is one form this resistance takes. Those who originated this burdensome religion—and yet rejected the version to which the Gentiles were converted—easily became the target of the resentment. One cannot dare to be hostile to one's all-powerful God. But one can to those who generated Him, to whom He revealed Himself and who caused others to accept Him. The Jewish God is invisible and unrepresentable, even unmentionable, a power beyond imagination, a law beyond scrutiny. He is universal, holding power over everybody and demanding obedience and worship from all. Nonetheless, He entered history and listened to, argued with, and chose the Jews—and the Jews alone. They are His people (though He must have known that He would be in for an endless argument). No wonder they also are the target of all those who resent His domination.

The Jewish God was both universal—the only real God

73

—and tribal: He had chosen the Jewish people and in exchange bound them to worship Him exclusively. Thus the Jews invented both monotheism and religious intolerance, or at least a passive form of it.* They had the only true religion, the only true promise; the only *real* God had chosen them—leaving the rest of the world to be comforted by false gods and messiahs. The Jews have suffered from their own invention ever since; but they have never given it up, for it is, after all, what makes the Jews Jewish. The Christians, when they became dominant, transformed the passive Jewish intolerance into active Christianity intolerance—of which the Jews became the first victim.

The ancients had many gods. These gods were powerful to an unspecified degree, and loved, hated, intrigued, and fought with each other, just as mortals did. They even competed for the devotion of the people who worshiped them. People thus had a choice as to which god to appeal to on each occasion—and they attributed their victories and defeats to the relative strength and benevolence of the tutelary deities invoked. No god had a monopoly: worshipers of one god recognized the existence of others, and did what was necessary to pay their respects and to conciliate them.

Each tribe or nation was quite willing to acknowledge not only the actual existence, but also the power of the gods of other tribes or nations, though every nation usually retained a preference for the home-grown deity. The recognition was quite sincere, for the ancients found the exis-

---

* The Jews did not actively object to what non-Jews believed. They merely thought the beliefs wrong—to us a very tolerant view. In the context of antiquity it seemed arrogant and ill-mannered. The passivity itself rested on arrogance.

tence of diverse tribal and specialized deities quite as natural as the existence of diverse tribes or occupations. It was regarded both as prudent and as a matter of common courtesy to honor the gods worshiped by others. One joined in the appropriate rituals and sacrifices when meeting with aliens who worshiped alien gods. Further, the gods served as political symbols. To accept the political domination of Rome did not mean that the subject peoples had to give up their customs, language, and culture. On the contrary, these were often accepted by the Romans. It meant an exchange: the subject people would add the Roman gods to their own and recognize them, at least as honored guests in their midst.

The vast religious tolerance prevalent in antiquity went far beyond what we conceive of as tolerance today. People not only granted the right to others to keep their own religion; they were convinced that the religion of the others was no less true than their own, their gods no less real—though each people hoped that their gods were the most powerful where it counted.

The Jewish religion did not fit into this framework at all. It made the Jews misfits in the world of the ancients and probably was one cause for the ultimate destruction of their country and their dispersal by the Romans.

The Romans treated the Jews tolerantly enough; but as victors, they insisted on those of their customs which symbolized submission to Roman power. Symbols of the Roman Empire—statues of Roman gods and semi-divine emperors —had been accepted everywhere else without difficulty. But to the Jews the statues were a blasphemous abomination, because of the Mosaic commandment that enjoins

75

against making "any likeness of anything," and against "bowing down thyself to them or serving them." Hence the Jews rebelled with religious zeal again and again, until their community was finally destroyed.

Later indeed the Jews destroyed the Roman framework that had made them misfits: their own religion, or much of it, was universally accepted, with the exception of the troublesome commandment against likenesses (although there have been iconoclastic moments in Christian history). But the Jews managed not to fit into the new Christian framework—so largely their own creation—any better. The Jewish Messiah the Gentiles recognized was not recognized as genuine by the Jews. He was not good enough for them —a view the Gentiles rather resented.* The gods the others believed in remained false gods to the Jews. He had revealed Himself to them only and He had chosen them alone. Which left the rest of the world out in the cold.

The religion of the Jews appeared to Gentiles absurd as well as outrageous; and ridiculous, too, if one considered that it was the religion of a small, insignificant, rustic nation, not distinguished for any major contribution to civilization. The Jewish views were certainly neither diplomatic nor endearing, and in the framework of antiquity, unreasonable, intolerant, and irrational. A tolerant and cultivated man, the emperor Julian Apostata, plaintively wrote of the Jews: "While striving to gratify their own God, they do not, at the same time, serve the others." This, according to Julian, was "their error." Politically, it was. And Jewish views were held with unaccustomed fanaticism. For the Jewish God did not serve His people. His people served Him—a wholly unancient conception.

* The Jews, of course, merely maintained that he was not genuine.

Not content with holding such absurd and intolerant beliefs—which, at best, could provoke only the ridicule, and, at worst, the hostility of all other peoples—the Jews rigidly refused even to tolerate the reasonable beliefs of others. The Romans had conquered them; but the Jews had the audacity to object to any attempt of the Romans to allow their soldiers to worship in their own fashion. All this in the name of what the Jews declared to be God's law against erecting false idols. It was as though the American Indians were to try to prohibit their conquerors from engaging in Christian worship in America. Such intolerance and apparent arrogance could not but provoke hostility. It did. Of course, in their view, the Jews merely objected to desecration of their holy sites. But try explaining that to a Roman.

Pre-Christian anti-Semitism was reinforced by a number of other Jewish traits. Their all-powerful God was invisible. He had forbidden the making of images not only of Himself but even of humans, let alone other gods. This prohibition helped to protect the belief in one God, for images soon come to be worshiped themselves, and different images would develop into different gods. Images of human beings could easily assume divine stature. And they could be used for magical purposes. Thus the Jewish religion differed from the others in kind; it did not compete with them, or recognize them, or have different rituals of the same genre. It was *sui generis,* a different kind of religion altogether, and it set its chosen people apart.

This "apartheid" was enjoined on the Jews as a moral duty, too. They were not meant to mingle with non-Jews and did not, to the extent to which they followed their religious leaders. To be sure, tribal pride and its enlarge-

77

ment, nationalism, as well as insistence on the superiority and preservation of one's culture, have always been with us. But these elements were religiously elaborated and adhered to by the Jews in far greater measure than by any other people—if such things can be measured. The Greeks did not think highly of "Barbarians" either. But the Jews went further and were more exclusive.

The Romans were hospitable to other cultures, religions, and peoples: not without grumbling, but still they were about as hospitable as present-day Americans. The Jews were stiff-necked, literal-minded, bothersome, and unrealistic. They refused to make the slightest concession, objecting even to Roman money because it bore the portraits of the emperors. In short, they gave no end of trouble —willfully, the Romans must have thought.

Most unpleasant, their invisible God not only insisted on being the one and only and all-powerful God—creator and lord of everything and the only rightful claimant to worship—He also developed into a moral God.

This, too, distinguished Him, and his worshipers, from the deities familiar to the pre-Christian world. These gods usually were personifications of the forces of nature, such as fertility; or of elements of the human personality, such as cunning; or of the social environment, such as war, craftsmanship, or art. Often these elements were blended, and the gods assumed magnified human personalities or natural powers; a moral element was present at times, but no more so than it is in most human beings. And one invoked the help of these gods by pleading, currying favor, and bribing them through sacrifices and through the fulfillment of their special demands.

78

The God of Israel, though only slowly shedding these elements, developed into something far more demanding, far harder to understand and obey. He developed from a natural into a truly supernatural spirit, and He demanded that his people follow moral rules and live a righteous life, in obedience to His law. Unlike the gods of others, who represented and accepted all parts of the human personality as they coexisted, fused, or struggled with each other, the God of the Jews came to represent a stern, dominating, and demanding paternal Superego—long before one of His chosen people invented, fathered (or at least baptized) the superego. The Jews exclusively worshiped a father God —not, as others did, a family of gods. This, too, set the Jews apart, not just because of their beliefs, but also because of the style of life that these beliefs enjoined.

The gods of the ancients were more or less helpful to, and protective of, their devotees, and were worshiped and sacrificed to for that reason. The Jews too had been chosen to receive certain promises from their God. But their choice involved incessant fidelity on the part of the Chosen, whose major preoccupation became the interpretation and fulfillment of their part of the bargain—the Law. Jewish life became God-centered, dominated by a priesthood which insisted on rituals and sacrifices, and by prophets who called on the people and their leaders to return to the spirit of Jehovah's laws; they interpreted all misfortunes as deserved punishments for disobedience, inflicted by an angry God. Jehovah exacted His end of the bargain and was not satisfied with anything but full value.

The Jews were constantly driven by their God, as His perpetual debtors. Their whole life revolved about doing His will, performing their duties to Him, attempting to satisfy Him. But speaking through His prophets, God spoke only of His displeasure. His Chosen People were not dutiful enough; they were ungrateful, faithless—in short, their God acted as an insatiable Superego. And the God of Israel punished His people accordingly with wars, floods, bondage, and famines, though saving them at the last moment, despite their sinfulness, because of the merits of one or two among them. He was infinitely merciful, this awe-inspiring father. He had to be, for in His eyes His people were infinitely guilty.

All this was hard to understand for the more easygoing ancients, and struck them as superstitious, a little ridiculous, ignorant, and unrealistic, as, indeed, it often strikes today's easygoing sophisticates, who may regard the whole business as "neurotic." The Jewish law seemed almost perverse in the value it placed on the invisible benefits of moral righteousness relative to the accessible pleasures of the senses. And yet, the Jews seemed uncanny. For there was no denying the moral fervor with which they stuck to their supernatural beliefs in the midst of a world concerned with quite different things. (In a similar way, the Roman Catholic Church, which certainly understands the power of moral ascendancy, has gained much from the almost eerie respect the ordinary man pays to the priest whose choice it is, on religious grounds alone, to live in celibacy.)

CHRISTIAN ANTI-SEMITISM

Pre-Christian anti-Semitism is explained largely by the Jews' contempt for Gentile gods and values, and by their continued insistence that they had a monopoly on the true God, and had been chosen by means of a special convenant. It is all right to love one's own God. It is certainly dangerous, however, to assert that the gods worshiped by others are false, and that their worshipers are being fooled —and to insist further that, unlike oneself, these worshipers of other gods were *not* chosen by the only true God, as evidenced by the unalterable fact of being born into the wrong group. Too bad for them.

When expressed by a small and powerless people, such as the Jews, such ideas cannot but lead to hostility and ridicule. When held by a dominant one, such ideas can lead to, or be used for, all the evils of racism. Which is what happened. The anti-Gentilism of the Jews was as real as—and preceded—the anti-Semitism of the Gentiles. But the Gentiles were materially stronger. The Jews were hoist by their own petard in more senses than one.

Christianity added elements to anti-Semitism which have their roots in the historical relationship between the Christian and the Jewish religions. Yet the Christian anti-Semites were no more conscious of the nature of these elements than the Jews. As was pre-Christian anti-Semitism, so Christian hostility to the Jews was overdetermined: in addition to the historical-religious, many other elements contributed to it; each of these, economic, religious, political, or psychological, might itself be a sufficient cause of anti-Semitism.

Christianity accused the Jews of having slain God. (As late as Vatican II, this accusation was seriously discussed, and cardinals of the Roman Catholic Church were on both sides of the question.) Deicide was attributed to the Jews because one of them, who proclaimed himself the Messiah and later was deified by His followers, was crucified in Jerusalem. The execution was carried out in the Roman manner (crucifixion was not a Jewish manner of execution) by the Roman troops occupying Jerusalem, probably because Jesus, as did other religious leaders of the time, appeared to the Romans as a dangerous subversive who might stir up the people against the Romans.

The Gospel tales—written long after the events—which have the arrest made and the death sentence pronounced at the behest of the Jewish Sanhedrin are scarcely plausible from a legal or historical viewpoint. The writers of the Gospels knew that Christianity was not making much headway among the Jews, whereas the number of Gentile converts, particularly Roman converts, was steadily mounting. It would have been undiplomatic, therefore, to saddle the Romans with deicide—while to accuse the Jews of hating the new God who came from their midst was to make that God more acceptable to the Romans. We don't know whether such considerations actually entered the minds of the Gospel writers. But these considerations would plausibly explain why the Jews, and not the Romans, were accused of what certainly must have been a Roman action—the condemnation and execution of Jesus.

It is quite likely, however, that the Jewish authorities did not greatly oppose the anti-subversive measures of the Romans. They, no less than the Romans, were opposed to whatever might stir up the people and lead them to attempt armed rebellion. For they saw—and history proved them right—that such a rebellion was quite hopeless. The prophets who arose from the people had little grasp of the distribution of power and relied, more than did the priestly hierarchy which dominated the Sanhedrin, on supposed divine revelation—which had led to disastrous adventures in the past. The many sects, the many enthusiasts, the many would-be prophets, the many fanatics and anti-Romans kept the established authorities, both Jewish and Roman, quite busy. If the Roman authorities wanted to avoid trouble, so did the Jewish authorities, for they feared the defeat which would—and in the end did—cost them the remnants of their independence. So much for the history of the matter, which is perhaps less important than the psychological genesis of anti-Semitism.

The Jews were accused of having killed God. Actually, the hostility to them may be based as much on having given birth to Him. For the Messiah, too, was a demanding and moral god who exacted sacrifices undreamed of before Christianity. Those making these sacrifices may well have turned their unconscious resentment not against the Savior —clearly an impossibility—but against His progenitors and relatives. After all, these relatives had mistreated the Savior, and murdered Him—which rationalizes any amount of hostility.

Further, the Jews remained faithful to their old God and repudiated His son. By this faithfulness, they show that they regard themselves still as chosen—and that the Christians worship a false god, a phony Messiah. Theirs remained a Father religion. Christianity became a Son religion. By their rejection of the Son, the Jews identified themselves with the Father, thus calling upon themselves all the resentment—all the ambivalence, at least—that comes with being identified with the Father.

83

But there is more. According to Freud, the Jews probably murdered not the Son, but God the Father—symbolized by Moses, the man who led them out of Egypt and out of the wilderness and gave them their Law. The grave of the father of Judaism was never found. According to Freud's speculation, the Jews in one of their many rebellions against his leadership actually murdered Moses. They never overcame their guilt feelings and became zealous and obedient sons to the father they had slain.

Even if Freud's speculation is no more than Freud's own fantasy, it seems a fantasy that meets, articulates, and explains, if not the facts, the conscious and unconscious fantasies of mankind and certainly of the Jews. The idea of parricide, and of expiation by the guilt-ridden sons through sacrifice of one of their own, was widespread among Oriental peoples, and quite popularly accepted among the Romans at the time the Gospels were created.

The Christians, through acknowledging the hereditary sin against God the Father, were purified of it and made, they thought, reacceptable to Him by their identification with the sacrifice of the Son. Jesus voluntarily allowed Himself to be slain. He was sent by His Father to redeem the world. The people who actually killed Him, according to the Gospels, however, did not accept their Oedipal guilt and, above all, the expiatory sacrifice of Jesus. Thus they were not redeemed. They continued to refuse purification, and thus to bear their sin, and, by their insistence that Jesus was a false Messiah, to add to it.

This insistence on the invalidity of Christ's redemptory sacrifice—for the sake of which the Jews suffered so much —could not but throw some doubt on the certainty of salvation. There were some—the Jews—that denied that Jesus had saved anyone; and they were willing themselves to die for the sake of this denial. Thus in Christian eyes the Jews became representatives of the offended, vengeful, and, according to them, unappeased Father.

In sort, the Jews repeated—however involuntarily and unwittingly—in the Christian world the arrogance which had caused the ancient world to hate them. They told the Christians that they had fallen for a phony Messiah, just as they had told the ancients that they worshiped false gods.* They, the Jews, alone were in possession of the true religion. What *chutzpah*.

But the Christians understandably were far more irked than the ancients. To the ancients, the Jewish religion was arrogant, foolish, and alien. To the Christians, it cast doubts on their most cherished beliefs. For many centuries Christians regarded the promise of life everlasting—paradise—as the most important thing on earth. Yet doubt was thrown on their belief in their salvation out of the same tradition from which the belief itself sprung, by the very people among whom the Messiah had arisen. An uncomfortable situation. It is not astonishing that the Jews were treated as one is always tempted to treat those who arouse doubts about one's own most cherished beliefs.

Things would have been different if one of them, Paul, had not decided that the Messiah rejected by the Jews could be accepted by the Gentiles, provided they would not first have to become Jews and be circumcised. The

---

* Perhaps "signified"—by their very existence and beliefs—is a better word than "told": the Jews did not proselytize, but their beliefs could not be ignored either.

story of salvation could be universalized. Paul proceeded to do this quite successfully.

Thus Gentiles accepted what the Jews had rejected and, in turn, rejected the people that did not want to give up being chosen. The Jews were burdened thenceforth not only with the sin which is the heritage of mankind, but also with their refusal to accept redemption, with slaying Him who wanted to redeem mankind, and finally with casting unrepentant doubt on the genuineness of the salvation vouchsafed the Gentiles.

The Christians now felt they could do to the representatives of the Father, in the name of the Son, what Christians would normally be punished for—were it not that the Son had removed the credentials of these representatives, the unredeemed Jews, and thus allowed them to be punished. To the Jews were attributed, unconsciously and sometimes consciously, all the things the sons fear: the father will castrate and kill them. And vengeance was taken on the Jews for these dreaded paternal intentions and fantasied deeds.

The Jews obdurately denied their share of guilt and their need for salvation and insisted that they had a special arrangement with God, the Father, which would save them and (the Christians thought) nobody else. If the Jews were right to any extent, the many renunciations that Christianity had imposed on its Gentile converts were in vain. The pleasures of this world would have been renounced for the sake of a paradise which was, after all, reserved for Jews.

No wonder the very existence of the Jews became a thorn in the side of Christianity. A useful thorn, as it were. For the Jews, by attracting hostility to themselves, solidified the identification of Christians with each other. Nothing does as much for internal solidarity as the existence of an external enemy. To the enemy, the group can attribute whatever it fears or detests in itself. Against him it can unite. Against him it can discharge hostility. As the chastity of nineteenth-century women required prostitutes, so the purity of Christian faith required Jews.

THE JEWISH CONSPIRACY: AN ANTI-SEMITIC FANTASY

In the primitive way in which they conceived it, the community of attitudes and characteristics among Jews was a myth invented by the Nazis for their own convenience. Radical parties, right or left, always simplify experience, however illegitimately, so as to manipulate a series of stereotypes in the end. It is their way of making life intelligible—and of proving that they could change it for the better and, therefore, ought to be on top.

Above all, Nazis, contrary to logic and fact, believed that the common attributes of the Jews (some real and some imagined for convenience) would lead to concerted actions and common purposes, to a conspiracy aimed at dominating and exploiting Gentiles. This "theory" was occasionally supported by faked documents—e.g., the "Protocols of the Elders of Zion."

Support for this sort of idea is produced by the general human inclination to attribute whatever is unpleasant or undesired to malevolent demons. With increasing secularization, the demons have been replaced by malevolent human groups—e.g., Jews, or capitalists. Witches form the bridge between these two versions. Thus the Germans, according to Hitler, did not lose World War I because they had been defeated by their enemies—an unacceptable blow to their superiority feelings—but because they were stabbed in the back by the Jews. And again, the Great Depression of the 1930's was caused by Wall Street Jews somehow acting in concert with Communists, who were also, it seems, Jews. And so on.

The Nazis were not very original in these fantasies. One model of the technique had been furnished—in secular form—by Karl Marx, a Jew. Of course, the Nazis are right: Jews are on all sides. The Nazis were wrong only in believing that they act in common: Germans, too, may be on all sides and so may women.

Marx attributed all the evils of the world to the capitalistic system; his less sophisticated followers (at times including Marx himelf) went on to attribute the evils of the world directly to the malevolence of capitalists. They humanized the theory, as Madison Avenue would say. Hitler blamed "the system," and "the Jews" who were supposed to be dominating it, for every wrong. Marx before him had blamed the capitalist system and "the capitalists" who were supposed to be dominating it. The "logical" structure is the same.

The socialist leader August Bebel—a German who died long before Hitler became known—was more accurate than he realized when he said: "Anti-Semitism is the socialism of the lower middle class." Psychologically it is indeed the equivalent of socialism, and takes its place for those to whom socialism is, or, as a result of its failures, becomes, unacceptable. (All utopian systems, and all systems supported by utopian enthusiasts, "fail": nothing ever lives up to our fantasy.) The symbols are different but the psychological essence of either ideology is the same: the evils of the world are presumed to be caused by a wrong system maintained by a small group who benefit from it and deliberately use the system to exploit the great majority. That majority—the people—are actually superior to the exploiters, either by virtue of their "race" and historical mission (Hitler) or by virtue of their "proletarian" descent, economic position, and historical mission (Marx).* The superior majority has the historical mission of eliminating the historically or racially corrupt minority, after which the millennium begins.

The origins of this conspiracy theory are found in primitive anthropomorphism. A traffic accident, or for that matter, a war, an economic depression, low farm prices, or the obsolescence of a given industry—all these things happen without being necessarily willed by anyone; yet they may injure or damage almost everyone, although in different degrees. As everyone pursues his course, the collision happens. As every farmer produces, prices fall, given certain circumstances. As each nation tries to achieve goals regarded as necessary by its government, it may collide with another nation pursuing its goals. An industry becomes obsolete because of technological developments not necessarily aimed at making it obsolete.

* Marx was considerably more sophisticated than Hitler and, above all, unlike Hitler, he was part of the rationalistic humanitarian tradition even though he repudiated it as sentimental in favor of science. Wherefore he appeals more to intellectuals. But his popular appeal has the same source as Hitler's: secularized Manichaean eschatology.

However, all of us find it hard to accept that anything really occurs without anyone willing it. Human beings usually have, or think they have, a purpose in their actions. They tend, therefore, to ascribe purposes to the world at large and to nature—and even more to actions undertaken or set in motion by fellow humans, such as wars or traffic collisions. It is hard for us to see that these may be simply the unintended result of deliberate acts. When these results are particularly unpleasant, they are ascribed to malevolent spirits and—with the secularization of our imagination—to malevolent people. Jews, for the reasons given, were easily the most likely malefactors.

Long after Marx, and not so long after Hitler, new versions of this ever-popular story, which in the childhood of the human race started with myths of demons and their human servants, abound. What else is C. Wright Mills' fascinating fable of the "power elite"? * In each of these versions, the believer has discovered that there are men more powerful than others, and that they often have more prestige and income than others, too. He then discovers that men outstanding in one activity are or become important in others, too: generals become corporate directors, directors of one corporation become directors of another, a man powerful in California may be influential in Washington and New York. The believer then concludes that these people, who have in common the fact that they are powerful, have little to divide them from each other, and that they share an overriding aim: to act in concert to

* Mills updated the matter: since the nation is more prosperous, it is harder for most people to believe that economic circumstances determine everything; they have found otherwise. Hence the "power elite" is not, in the main, an economic class. It is a status group.

their advantage and to the detriment of the less powerful. And that explains whatever happens that is unpleasant. "They" done it, whatever it is: started the war, or lost it . . . caused the depression, or the inflation . . . brought about the imperialistic expansion, or the cowardly retrenchment.

Just as Hitler and C. Wright Mills did, I too have come to the conclusion that we are dominated and exploited by a "power elite." Only, unlike my fellow scholars, I don't identify the members as either rich or Jewish. Upon extensive research, I found that we are dominated by men wearing glasses; they succeed in getting each other into corporate directorships, become generals, music critics, stockbrokers, senators, Supreme Court justices, and cabinet members. They conspire against anyone not shortsighted. I can prove that easily. (For statistical tables about eyeglasses worn by men in leading positions, which clearly demonstrate my theory, see Appendix.)*

Until Hitler nearly killed them all, the Jews were excellent targets for this sort of thing. To Gentiles, they were strange and uncanny: in, but not really accepted as part of, the society in which they lived. They were active, often reached outstanding positions, yet were different and therefore did not quite belong. And they certainly had something in common that could not be denied and that differentiated them: they were Jews. It is as though they were some kind of family mysterious to nonmembers, some kind of network with an eerie communications system, omnipresent, powerful, sinister, and yet almost anony-

---

* I haven't decided yet about wearers of sunglasses, probably a rival power elite. Still waiting for a grant to work on that.

mous at the center of the body politic. Were they not on all sides? Did they not therefore cause everything? It is the "therefore," of course, that constitutes the fallacy: men with glasses are prominent on all sides but do not "therefore" act in common to cause everything. Even if people have things in common, it does not follow that they will act in common, let alone conspire. But it's too nice a theory just to drop.

Among many widely recognized and ambivalently admired characteristics of the Jews are a desire for education, a low rate of alcoholism, an almost invisible rate of what we now call juvenile delinquency ("radical" activity is the Jewish form of defying authority). These characteristics do not make the anti-Semites like Jews—on the contrary. After all, such traits can be explained: the desire for education is part of Jewish pushiness and of the plan for world domination; if you are engaged in a serious conspiracy, you can't afford to get drunk—*in vino veritas:* people who have so much to hide won't dare get drunk; and there is no need for juvenile delinquency if you, together with your parents, are conspiring to do in the rest of the world.

The interesting thing is that all of these paranoid fantasies are also negative versions of half-truths: Jews are ambitious; they have messianic dreams; and their abstemiousness may have something to do with fear of baring guilty secrets to a hostile world. These semiconscious Jewish feelings are perceived by anti-Semites and projected as realities. Thus, anti-Semitism on the psychological level is the product of a cooperative effort involving Jews and their enemies; on a rational level it is nonsense, a pseudo-explanation of history which, particularly in time of distress, helps people shift the blame from themselves.

This nonsense was accepted by enough people to make possible the horrors of concentration camps and the murder of six million Jews. It is hard to believe in God; it is harder still to believe in human rationality.

6

Two Kinds of Discrimination: Jews and Negroes

WHEN Jews were finally accepted into American society, they were allowed to succeed or fail according to their individual merits as others did—almost. They mostly succeeded.

Until the Second World War, some extra merit was still required for promotion and recognition to come to Jews. Their achievement had to be both undeniable and extraordinary to gain the recognition that might come to Gentiles of ordinary merit. Jewish lawyers became Supreme Court justices in spite of Jewish origin; Jewish physicians became members of medical faculties even though Jewish; Jewish scholars attained professorial rank despite being Jews. It would be tedious to prolong the listing, and redundant, as well as pedantic, to document the point. Since Jews were held to be in some general way inferior—a survival of the historical Christian viewpoint, which enabled Gentiles to look upon them as unredeemed social pariahs—special gifts, merits, or abilities were required to offset the assumed inferiority: to be granted parity, Jews had to be superior to their peers.

The extra barriers Jews had to overcome for promotion and recognition, and the extra merits and efforts required to do so, were—need it be said?—inequitable. Nonetheless, the effect, unintended and unanticipated by those who built barriers to keep out Jews, to make sure that their status remained inferior, was to create an aura of superiority which ever since has surrounded Jews.

Over a fairly long period, only Jews who actually were quite superior to their professional or scholarly peers obtained recognition and promotion. Thus Jews achieved prominent positions which made them highly visible to Gentiles only if they actually were superior to their Gentile colleagues. Unavoidably Jews came to be regarded as usually having abilities superior to those of Gentiles.*

The college student would find that, on the whole, his Jewish professors were better than his Gentile professors: they had to be, to become professors. The effects of discrimination against Jews in other professions and activities were analogous: they always had to be better qualified than Gentiles to achieve the same rank. The resulting visible superiority was quite naturally linked with Jewishness by Gentile observers. In the end the discriminatory selection, prompted by the wish to keep Jews in an inferior position, created an image of Jewish intellectual superiority. The ungifted among Jews were hardly visible to the Gentile world, although they are the majority of Jews, as they are in any other group.

Again, it was Gentile pressure and Gentile laws that

---

* They may actually have superior abilities in some respects, as suggested in Chapter One. But the selection process described above is an independent source of the belief in their superiority.

drove Jews into the cities, and into occupations such as money lending and international trade, which, though necessary, useful, and profitable, were undertaken by Gentiles only with reluctance and in some cases were regarded as sinful by them. With the development of an industrial society, their specialization in these occupations gave Jews an indirect power. This power seemed mysterious—inconsistent as it was with their low social position and their lack of political power. The mystery added to their ambivalent prestige. Most important, their specialization and their lack of a vested interest in the agricultural and feudal order made the adjustment of Jews to the modern, urban, industrial world easier than that of any other group—and, therefore, helped them play a leading role in it. This development, largely due to discrimination against them, in the end added as well to the belief in the superiority of Jews.

As might be expected, the public image of Jewish cleverness and superiority which was unwittingly created, or at least confirmed, by anti-Semitic practices, had ambivalent effects. In Germany, it contributed to a defensive reaction: let us kill those who, by possibly being superior, may confront us with our own inadequacy and threaten our dominant position as well as our feeling of superiority. In the United States, which does not have a homogeneous group that feels threatened (and where the threat to WASPs comes from more than one quarter), the reaction has been more along the lines of: if you can't beat them, join them. The joining has accelerated in the last few decades.

Thus, Walter Kerr, in the *New York Times* (April 14, 1968) discussed Leo Rosten's *Education of H*Y*M*A*N K*A*P*L*A*N,* a musical based on short stories Rosten published in the *New Yorker* magazine some thirty years ago.

The musical follows the stories; it affectionately celebrates the Americanization, through education, of a well-meaning, clever, over-eager, naïve, and somewhat overbearing Jewish immigrant. Kerr points out that Rosten celebrates the Jewish infusion into the melting pot—the difficulties his Jewish immigrants eagerly try to overcome in adapting themselves to a WASPish America.

> As things stand, Mr. Parkhill is the American of the piece, and the immigrants are the good folk who are trying to make themselves over in his likeness. They wish to pronounce "w" as he does, read as he does, hear as he does, think as he does. He, cleancut and confident, is no doubt what we have come to call a Wasp. A good and earnest and likeable Wasp. He is us, and they are they, waiting to become us.

But, Mr. Kerr goes on, the situation is no longer relevant; we understand it only with an effort now. It is no longer our experience. On the contrary:

> Today, only 25 years later, the immigrants—above all the Jewish immigrants—seem more American than he does. They are faces and voices and inflections of thought that seem most familiar to us, literally second nature; he is the odd ball, the stranger, the fossil. We glance at him, a bit startled, and say to ourselves, "Where did he go?" We remember him: pale, poised, neatly dressed, briskly sure of himself. And we see him as an outsider, an outlander, a reasonably noble breed in the act of vanishing. He is performing tonight as a molder of minds, but he is no longer in any sense the mold we have in mind. He has stopped being representative, and we didn't notice it until this minute. Not so emphatically anyway.

A vast transition has reversed what we are looking at. It's not just a matter of having been so exposed to Jewish entertainers and Jewish novelists that their tricks of rhythm have curled up in everyone's ears and come to feel at home there. That's happened, all right. Collecting Yiddish words and dropping them into Madison Avenue sentences has been fashionable for a long time now, so fashionable that it, too, is out of date. The Gentile who can't invert his sentence structure to make it sound pleasantly Jewish probably doesn't exist outside of Kansas. (How is it in Kansas? I don't know.)

Everybody today has a Jewish mother, whether she is Irish or whatnot. And the Gentile, or for that matter the Jew, who now settles for a fast "all right already" or a sentence beginning with "So" in order to display his credentials as a sophisticate is all too plainly not a sophisticate. That's baby talk, affectation, even less than skin deep.

This is particularly true for literature:

What has happened since World War II is that the American sensibility itself has become in part Jewish, perhaps nearly as much Jewish as it is anything else. And this is nothing so superficial as sympathetic identification (because so many Jews were killed) or a playful Gentile gesture of friendliness (because quirks of speech can be charming). It goes right to the bone, all the way in. The literate American mind has come in some measure to think Jewish, to respond Jewishly. It has been taught to, and it was ready to. After the entertainers and the novelists came the Jewish critics, politicians, theologians. Critics and politicians and theologians are by profession molders: they form ways of seeing.*

One may quibble about the extent, the pervasiveness, and the persistence of the development Mr. Kerr describes.†

* © 1969 by The New York Times Company. Reprinted by permission.
† See Chapter 8.

But can one deny it? In America the fear of and the desire for the (true or imagined) Jewish superiority has been dealt with by absorbing the Jews, making them part of the American self-image. We have given a Jewish flavor to whatever was cooked in the melting pot. Other ingredients were more sizable. But the Jews were the spice that came to dominate the flavor most of the time.

At present, we witness the attempts of Negroes to be fully accepted as equals in America, to be considered each on his individual merits alone. As their history differs from Jewish history, so does the attempt of Negroes to be recognized as equals in America differ from that of Jews; and so does the response.

Negroes are neither recent nor voluntary immigrants. They were brought to America forcibly; they were oppressed; they were made to live in, but not allowed to be of, the society which used them for centuries. Unlike Jews, they lived in rural areas far from the city slums to which they now are migrating. In these "ghettos" they engage in occupations most often shunned by whites. But these are not now finance and commerce—the occupations Gentiles left to Jews—but low-paying, menial jobs with little chance for advancement or independence. The Gentile leftovers which the Jews had to be content with turned out to be the mainstays of the age that was to come. But what was left for Negroes was whatever tended to become obsolete and actually had been left by whites for newer and better occupations.

Most important, the tribal cultures Negroes possessed, even their language, as well as their religion, were destroyed in slavery. The Negro family itself was impaired. Had they not been destroyed, their original tribal cultures still could not have prepared Negroes for the civilization to which they were suddenly and forcibly removed. The absence of a viable tradition of any endogenous culture of their own, and their low status in American society, often led to a self-image of inadequacy which reduces and distorts motivation even when opportunity is present.

The present attempt of Negroes to enter American society, unlike that of other groups, is bitter and resentful as often as eager, violent as often as diligent. The reaction of the white environment also differs. Often it is guilt-ridden; in the past it was openly hostile; and it threatens to become so once more as the lower middle classes feel threatened by Negroes, even if that threat more often flows from the rhetoric of militants than from any actual power shift. For a long time, the relation between Negroes and whites is likely to be felt, at best, as an antagonistic symbiosis.

Now successful and accepted, Jews are quite frequently in positions to lead; and they feel guilty about Negroes. Unlike the guilt feelings of WASPs, those of Jews do not spring from having been oppressors in the past, but rather from having been oppressed as well. Jews identify with the oppressed and deprived Negro treated by his white environment in a way all too familiar to them—a way which cannot but recall the memory of their own oppression, deprivation, and ghettoization. Now that they are successful, Jews feel that they have the obligation to help those who suffer, as they did, from discrimination; those who are considered, as the Jews were, as inferior; those who are, as they were, oppressed and held in contempt; those who so often are stereotyped, to whom so many unfavorable characteristics are ascribed, as they were to Jews.

The identification, to be sure, is topological only: Negroes occupy a social spot once occupied by Jews (often they actually occupy the formerly Jewish areas of cities); they do not resemble Jews in background, attitude, character, or characteristics. Above all, they lack the cohesive culture, the religion, the self-image Jews managed to create and preserve, and their family relationship to Christian culture. Never mind; the guilt feeling is genuine enough. Yet, however necessary it may be as motivation, I do not think that this Jewish guilt feeling (shared by many non-Jews as well) is a useful guide to action. On the contrary, the actions prompted by it threaten to make matters worse—particularly "reverse discrimination": discrimination in favor of Negroes. Many Negroes, and nearly all their spokesmen, now claim this favorable discrimination as a right.

Jews, as mentioned, had to be better than Gentiles to attain equal rank, to be promoted in spite of being Jewish. Thus the Jews who became notable and were regarded as representative, who created the public image, not to say the stereotype, were usually better qualified than their Gentile colleagues. "Reverse discrimination," however, means that Negroes often are promoted not *despite* being Negroes, but *because* they are, and regardless of merit. Because they are Negroes they are accepted as students, even when less qualified than whites, and given scholarships over white competitors. Perhaps such "compensatory opportunity" can be justified when it is combined with special help to allow the students selected to catch up with their

101

fellow students—when they are qualified except for lack of opportunity; but not when they are not.

However, Negroes are also sought out and asked to join faculties over more qualified white competitors. Anyone familiar with the situation knows that colleges look high and low for Negro students and faculty members and accept them over better qualified white ones. This holds not only for universities, but for many institutions, for corporations, and for many high status jobs. "Reverse discrimination" may have contributed to the situation referred to in the Report of the National Advisory Commission on Civil Disorders, named by President Johnson to investigate the 1967 riots:

> . . . the proportion of Negroes employed in high-skill high-status and well-paying jobs, rose faster than the comparable proportion among whites from 1960 to 1966.*

Justices Cardozo, Brandeis, and Frankfurter became justices of the Supreme Court in spite of being Jewish. Thurgood Marshall became Mr. Justice Marshall *because* he is Negro. He is a competent lawyer. No one ever accused him of being an outstanding jurist.†

To be sure, politics has often played a role in nomina-

---

* The Census Bureau also found that from 1959 to 1967 the median income of white families rose 46.6%, that of Negro families 76.2%; nonetheless a far higher (though diminishing) proportion of Negroes remain poor than of whites (nearly one-third of all Negro families are poor and less than 10% of all white families).

† The purely political process is, surprisingly, an exception. Although ethnic selection has been traditionally part of it, Mr. Brooke seems to have become Senator from Massachusetts neither because of, nor despite, his skin color—or perhaps both because of *and* despite.

tions to the Supreme Court. More than one jurist was named for political reasons when many better qualified lawyers were overlooked. One may argue that since there was for so long a time discrimination in favor of WASPs, some discrimination in favor of blacks can be justified. It is a dubious argument, appealing more to politicians, for whom two wrongs offset each other, than to the philosopher, for whom they do not make a right. In terms of equity, the argument runs as follows: well-connected whites in the past have often gained positions over more qualified competitors in corporations and elsewhere. Negroes have no such connections. Why not give them a similar opportunity by granting them preference over whites, even over more qualified ones?

Such an argument treats Negroes and whites as groups with competing claims to be balanced, and not as individuals whose individual qualifications ought to be considered paramount. Past practice may make the disregard for individual qualifications in favor of group discrimination seem equitable. But it reinforces rather than eliminates group discrimination and, despite apparent advantages, harms the members of all groups. Injustice—even when compensatory —is never in the social interest.

The actual, present, and future effects are more important than the intended equity of compensatory "reverse discrimination." To offset past deprivations, we now place Negroes in positions and ranks for which, as they are being placed, they are less qualified than competing whites. Could the effects of this "reverse discrimination" damage the

Negroes who are to be favored? What specific effects can we expect on

a) the self-image of Negroes?

b) the attitude of whites toward Negroes and of Negroes toward whites?

c) the image of Negroes among whites?

a) Negroes will not be able to overlook for long that they are being promoted in a discriminatory fashion. Even though the discrimination be in their favor, they are still not being treated in terms of individual merit, or qualifications, but as members of a group. Unlike Jews, they cannot have the feeling that their individual abilities have, in each particular case, overcome and defeated the prejudice against the group. On the contrary, they must be aware that they may be promoted not because of individual qualifications but, regardless of merit, because they are Negroes. They are reduced to members of a group. Thus, a Negro who is actually as well qualified as his white colleagues will never be sure whether he is promoted because of his individual qualifications, or to make up for the prejudice against his group by singling out members for especially favorable (discriminatory) treatment.

This doubt will not help the self-image even of those Negroes who are as well or better qualified than whites— while those who are not will come to believe that a job, and a status, is owed them as Negroes, regardless of qualifications. Which will not strengthen their motivation to acquire qualifications.

b) Some whites will resent favorable treatment given Negroes as such when it means disadvantages for whites of equal or superior merit. However, the need for qualified people in most occupations is so great that few whites will actually suffer. Hence this effect may be regarded as materially negligible. Psychologically, however, it is not negligible at all: it will help rationalize and intensify resentments against Negroes originating elsewhere. It will strengthen prejudice. Among Negroes, "reverse discrimination" will foster a "dependent attitude" which demands advantages, and refuses to achieve them realistically by acquiring relevant qualifications.

c) The effect of discrimination *in favor* of Negroes on the image of Negroes among whites will be disastrous—different, but ultimately not better than the effect of discrimination *against* Negroes. Preferential treatment of Negroes, placement in positions for which they are less qualified than white competitors, means that among students and faculties and in the professions, there will be more Negroes than before—and that on the average they will be less well qualified than the majority of their white colleagues. This disparity cannot remain hidden for long to either Negroes or whites. Ultimately, just as the Jewish image was largely created by the superiority of the most visible Jews to Gentile colleagues, as perceived by them and by clients, patients, and students, so the Negro image will be influenced strongly by the inferiority of the most visible Negroes to white colleagues, as perceived by them and by clients, patients, and students.

The well-meant present policies of the friends of Negroes certainly yield advantages, in the short run, both to the individual Negroes who benefit and to the guilt-ridden consciences of their benefactors. But the long-range effects are likely to be calamitous for the Negro people. Groups of Negroes may profit; Negroes as a group will suffer. Their self-image of inferiority to whites and of inadequacy will be reinforced. And the whites' image of Negroes as inferior, as less well qualified for most things than whites, will be confirmed.

It does not do justice to Negroes to discriminate against them. Neither does it do justice to them to discriminate in favor of Negroes. In promoting individuals, a just society must disregard anything other than the comparative qualifications of each individual for the rank to which he aspires. All irrelevant discrimination—discrimination based on group membership or other qualities not relevant to the task at hand—must be avoided, be it in favor of or against any particular group.* If irrelevant discrimination has occurred in the past, the reverse irrelevant discrimination does not offset it; it adds to it.

Charity and benevolence, the attempt to make up for past suffering, have their place. A society without them will not be a good society. But nothing can take the place of justice. A society that neglects justice in favor of charity becomes unjust, and ultimately uncharitable as well. The first reaction of those who feel themselves unjustly treated will be vindictive harshness; they will ignore even the proper claims of charity.

Charity and love are virtues separate from (if related to) justice. A society must not only strive toward virtue; it must strive toward the right order of virtues. Nothing prevents the private citizen, and at times even his govern-

---

* Group membership may be relevant to election for political offices which should give representation to groups, among other things.

106

ment, from helping Negroes to achieve qualifications and from helping them according to their need. If the need of Negroes is greater than that of others, so should the help be. Love discriminates in favor of preferences, and charity discriminates in favor of needs. But in promotion for any one rank, the public virtue of justice must prevail. Only the qualifications actually attained should count. To ignore this simple rule, to slight justice in favor of charity, distorts the social order; and it will injure the recipients of favor above all others. Negroes once more will be made to suffer —this time from the guilt-ridden beneficence of their well-wishers.

NEGRO ANTI-SEMITISM

Negroes are naturally resentful of whites: whites have what Negroes want—income, power, prestige, and, so it seems, the feeling of security, of adequacy, of pride that goes with all this. Do they? I doubt it. But to Negroes it looks as though whites do, which is what matters. They resent it.

This Negro resentment is often directed particularly against Jews. The most obvious reason is that Jews are the whites with whom the urban Negroes—the most resentful, most articulate, and most militant Negroes—are most frequently in contact. The Jewish landlord continued to own property after his Jewish tenants were replaced by Negro tenants; the Jewish storekeeper continued to keep the store after his Jewish customers moved away and were replaced by Negro customers. They are the most obvious and concrete targets for the Negro ghetto dweller dissatisfied with the housing and the merchandise available to him. He is resentful of the white world, of which the Jews become the most visible representatives. They also furnish many of the social workers whom Negroes naturally resent, and many of the teachers who do not succeed in teaching Negro children as much as they might learn.

Far from obviating Negro anti-Semitism, the disproportionately great number of Jews among the civil rights workers who try to help Negroes tends, at least in the short run, to intensify it. Negroes want to achieve their own "liberation"; they need and accept, but unavoidably resent, the help they are getting. However much needed, that help indicates, by being needed, their own inadequacy. Or so they feel. This is not surprising. It has always been harder to accept charity than to give it. The resentment of one's own need and dependence is often shifted to the donor; so are the infantile demands that are associated with the dependence: why not more? why not get everything? The very presence of Jews, of well-educated, intelligent, and helpful persons who, not being in need themselves, can afford to be helpful, necessarily makes them a target of the resentment of the Negroes whom they help: the helpers have what the helped want; more important, they are what he aspires to, and their generosity makes them even more superior and, therefore, more resented.

Sophisticated Jews may understand and forgive—or, at least, persist. But many Jews are baffled: here these militants beat up the Jewish teacher who is trying to help their kids and has tried harder than his non-Jewish colleagues.

"My cousin Lenny went down South when it counted, to help Negroes at the risk of being shot by enraged white racists. He is risking his life once more. Now he risks being shot by enraged black racists who discount everything he stood for and did, and does. It was not enough; or was it too much?"

He is attacked, some Jews say rather apologetically—they are in the habit of apologizing—not as a Jew but as a white man. After all, he is white even though Jewish, and Negroes don't discriminate: white is white.

Not quite. Negro militants resent all whites—as they proclaim—including, of course, Jews; but they also resent Jews as such.

Jews are a conspicuously successful American minority. They have it made. Negroes have not. Naturally the resentment of the unsuccessful is directed against the successful minority, against those who were badly off, too, but made it—against those who serve almost as a living reproach, illustrating failure by contrast. Such a comparison would be irrational for many reasons, but resentment is an emotion before it is a thought. And Negroes now are the only ones who can permit their resentment to take an anti-Semitic direction.

Themselves an oppressed minority, Negroes are on the way to becoming the only certified kosher anti-Semites: WASPs, after Hitler, cannot afford any public display of even the most harmless social form of anti-Semitism.

On the other hand, a significant number of Jewish students went on strike at NYU to protest the firing—not the hiring—of John F. Hatchett,* a Negro, whose speeches finally became too anti-Semitic even for those who had

---

* Hatchett was hired by NYU as director of an institute for black NYU students and studies. Both the institute and the selection of the director were responses to minority student demands. The purpose was to satisfy minority ambitions and to achieve racial peace. Hatchett defeated this last purpose by delivering anti-Semitic speeches to NYU students.

hired him in the first place. Yet, despite some curious publications, he had been certified kosher by none other than former Justice Arthur Goldberg. Whereupon he made more racist speeches, complaining about the injustice of the Jews—while actually suffering from their excessive charity. Had he been white, he would not have had a chance. As it is, he may now make a living addressing audiences on the injustices suffered by his race.

Will Jewish indulgence reduce, or foster Negro anti-Semitism? Negro resentment is prompted by too much evidence of Jewish guilt feeling. For Jews feel guilty about their own success, or at least act as though they do. Quite often they are willing to support even the most unrealistic and silly demands of Negroes simply because they are Negro demands. Jews, even when (or because) rich, still tend to identify with the poor—they had been poor. Jews, though powerful, tend to identify with the powerless and persecuted—they had been powerless and persecuted. Thus to Jews, Negroes appear to be their own former selves. They identify if only because Negroes are in the position relative to whites in which Jews were relative to Gentiles. But Negroes do not identify with the rich and powerful Jews. They merely resent them and, above all, their generosity: the very symbol of the resented superiority.

Finally, and perhaps most importantly, confused by their guilt feelings, Jews cannot grasp that many Negro demands are simply irrational: explainable psychologically, they make no sense in reality terms. Liberals, and most conspicuously Jewish liberals, are willing to grant Negro demands, sometimes just ones and sometimes unreasonable ones; and to do so regardless of the means by which the demands are advanced.

But the most conspicuously militant Negroes do not want concessions, though they ask for them. Whenever something is granted, they want more or something else, for the simple reason that they do not want to be *given* anything—they want a fight. The object of the fight is less important than the process of fighting for it, and the pride that comes from having obtained something through power, even violence, rather than through the generosity of others.

The need to fight arises from feelings of humiliation and inadequacy which generate anger, an anger that can be discharged only in a fight that restores pride and a feeling of adequacy. Things given do not satisfy. Only things taken do. Concessions do not help. Only victories do. Here, for once, the medium has become the message.

By now the demoralization wrought by external events has made many Negroes prone to hysteria—it has become an internal condition not easily corrected by external changes, and certainly not immediately. With this hysteria there goes some dissociation from reality and much irrationality, many delusive dreams of power and glory. Jews—rationalists *par excellence*—find it hard to grasp the fact that they are not called upon to negotiate, to concede, to grant, to give; that Negroes want above all to discharge their anger, and have contempt for those who, instead of permitting it to be discharged, try to circumvent the anger by what Negroes feel are bribes. They don't want to be cheated out of it.

This is not the place to discuss the cause and remedies for Negro anger. But one thing should be clear: it is not any longer a rational matter; it must be discharged. Jews who insist on treating this anger as though it could be assuaged by concessions are most likely to become its targets. People who want to fight respect others who do, not those who tell them that they can have what they want without the fight they want most of all.

To illustrate, Negroes are agitating to be admitted and integrated into colleges and schools. But whenever this is obtained, or in the process of being obtained, Negroes insist on segregation, on their own dormitories, classes, and, finally, "institutes." They want Negro culture taught by blacks to blacks—just as the Nazis felt that Jews could not teach Germans about German culture. They want control over hiring and firing of teachers and over standards and, therewith, degrees. But were they to obtain such control, the degree would not be a Harvard degree, but a degree from an Afro-American Studies Institute, albeit at Harvard. Its value would be questionable. Negro-controlled colleges exist now, and their students suffer from their frequently low academic standards. Will a wholly Negro-controlled institute at Harvard or Cornell fare any better? Yet Jews are in the forefront of those wishing to indulge the self-defeating and unreasonable demands of Negro militants.

When rationalized by "progressive" ideologies, the Jewish guilt feeling borders on the absurd and, not infrequently, the suicidal. Thus, I. F. Stone, a leading contributor to the *New York Review of Books,* wrote: "It will not hurt us Jews to swallow a few insults from overwrought blacks." Black anti-Semitism is forgivable (unlike, say, Irish or WASPish anti-Semitism). Although worse than some, Stone is not alone.*

There are no justifications for black anti-Semitism, or

---

* S.D.S., the student radical group, not only opposes Israel but supports *Al Fatah,* the main Arab guerrilla group. About half of S.D.S. consists of Jews. It is hard to admire them.

for any other variety, although there are explanations. Paradoxically, far from being anti-white, as apologists maintain, black anti-Semitism is an attempt to identify with whites by imitating some of their worst features, not necessarily as they exist, but as the imitators imagine them. Anti-Semitism is not an African trait. Negroes learned it from American whites. The Arabs were the traditional enemies of the African Negroes. They, not the Jews, were slave traders. However, American Negro militants—cheered on by their Jewish supporters—are pro-Arab, anti-Israel. In the United States itself, if Negroes have reason to be more hostile to one nationality than to another, certainly the Jews deserve the least hostility. They were not plantation owners. They did not engage in lynching—indeed, occasionally, they were among the lynched. In recent times Jews more than any other group have pressed for the advancement of Negroes, and in 1968 a smaller proportion of Jews than of members of any other white group voted for Wallace, the most clearly anti-Negro candidate.

Obviously Negro militants are anti-Semitic because of Jewish friendliness, weakness, and encouragement, not because of Jewish hostility. They can count on the Jews to remain their friends. Jews are too "progressive" to react otherwise. The tactic which involved "to swallow a few insults" was so unavoidable in the past that it still seems acceptable to many Jews, particularly when these insults come from the "left." But is it necessary or helpful to Jews, or to the political education of Negroes, to teach them that Jews can be singled out for hostility—with impunity?

The matter does not stop at insults. Negro militants demand "quotas" for Negroes wherever they can. Now in some activities, such as the building trades from which Negroes have been unfairly excluded for years, this might be a reasonable method of entry. But in other activities the merit system has actually prevailed for some time now. In higher education, for instance, after the quota system once used to restrict the number of Jews—the *numerus clausus*—was abolished, a genuine merit system replaced it. As a result, Jews are statistically overrepresented among both teachers and students.

Negro militants now insist on quota systems to increase the number of Negroes, independently of qualifications. Ultimately Jews would have to bear the burden of it. If colleges will have 11 per cent Negro students—approximately the proportion of Negroes in the population—why should they have more than 3 per cent Jewish students (and professors), approximately the proportion of Jews in the population? Once positions are assigned by quota, and not by merit, this seems just. Yet Jews are more prominent in supporting Negro demands for academic quotas than for quotas in the building trades. And Negro militants are more militant with academic opponents than with union leaders. They select the most indulgent, not the most harmful opponents.

Obviously, the merit principle for which Jews fought so hard does benefit them. But society also benefits when positions are distributed according to competence rather than according to race. Possibly this is not a good or feasible idea in political matters. Wherefore in these matters people are allowed to decide according to any criterion they prefer, and competence does not necessarily count. But elsewhere, and particularly in education, it has finally and rightly counted. Yet Jewish students and professors are now cheering on Negro militants in their demand for quotas.

Although well endowed with it, Jews are no more *dominated* by their intelligence than other people; they often use it to rationalize their emotions. Here the identification with the underdog seems to go beyond all reason, and the actions it suggests to Jews are undertaken in spite of intelligence.

7

Jewish Radicals
and Jewish Hippies

BY VIRTUE of their history and of the character shaped by it, Jews are vulnerable to radical ideas. Utopian dreams, millennial prophecies, and messianic expectations are as much part of their cultural heritage as is the practical worldly attitude for which they are so well known. In an oppressive environment, their utopianism took an other-worldly, religious form. With emancipation, Jews have tried to influence their actual environment, in this world. But they have not given up their dreams. Many have become reformers; many others have become radicals.

Of all groups dissatisfied with the quality of their life, and rebellious, the Jews are most prone to expectations of radical change. They have indulged such hopes since their Babylonian captivity, and they won't be robbed of them by the comforts and conveniences of their second "captivity" in Babylon, the all-too-well-named New York suburb. Usually the hoped-for radical change has involved a return to the past, to Jerusalem, to paradise. But the return is metaphorical now: American Jews refrain from going to the Promised Land; the American fleshpots are safer and more nourishing. Yet they go on feeling exiled, go on chanting: "Next year in Jerusalem." Their nonreligious children act out the same ritual, but replace exile with capitalism, Jerusalem with a sort of populist anarcho-socialism reminiscent of the *Narodniki* of Czarist Russia.

Politically most Jews are liberals; some are radicals; a few are conservatives.* The radicals concern us here. They make the most noise.

The liberals are vaguely for more egalitarian measures and for more welfare and civil rights. They are indulgent toward the radicals. The conservatives stress individual intiative and its rewards, and are distressed by taxes, welfare measures, and too many restrictions on property rights; they are impatient with radicals. Both liberal and conservative Jews uphold the system of institutions in which they live, though wishing for some reform from the left or right.

The radicals do not. They want to abolish some or all American institutions—the kind of democracy to which Americans are accustomed, its economic, political, judicial, and academic institutions—to replace them with something radically different.

Past radicals had fairly specific ideas about the new institutions they favored. Today's radicals are vague and offer generalized slogans more often than specific programs.

---

* The 1968 presidential election demonstrated once more how firmly liberal Jews are. In that election, the high income groups voted for Nixon (63 per cent) as did the professional and college-educated groups (54 per cent). On the other hand, Negroes (94 per cent) and Puerto Ricans (81 per cent) voted for Humphrey. So did the Jews (81 per cent). Although in a higher income and education bracket than any other group, they voted as those in the lowest income and education brackets did.

They know what they are against though: practically everything their parents have done. To get rid of the present social system, some radicals would not always shun violence; and all radicals favor at least some degree of subversion. Mostly the violence is to be invited by resisting "passively," so as to provoke others. Some radicals, however, are willing to initiate violence themselves.

Although very few Jews are radicals, very many radicals are Jews: out of one hundred Jews, five may be radicals, but out of ten radicals five are likely to be Jewish. Thus it is incorrect to say that a disproportionate number of Jews are radicals but quite correct to say that a disproportionate number of radicals are Jews. This was so in the past, and it has not changed. What attracts them so disproportionately to radical causes?

After all, the Jews are no longer oppressed by the government—an oppression which led some Jews to radicalism in Czarist Russia. Nor do they any longer work in the sweatshops and live in the slums of America—conditions that helped keep the radical tradition alive in the new country. Many Jews live in prosperous suburbs, often in an opulent style. Although most Jews are not rich, and most rich people are not Jewish, the number of financially successful Jews is as disproportionate as is that of radical Jews. In short, they never had it so good. Why, then, are so many among the radically dissatisfied Jewish?

It helps to remember that many affluent Jews are children of poor and radical Jews who have reconciled themselves to existing society enough to do well in it, but not enough not to feel guilty about doing well, about "betraying" their own youthful radical ideas and, perhaps, their poverty. When they were poor, they repudiated the goal—which then seemed unattainable—of becoming rich as individuals. They were going to "change the system" instead. They didn't; and they did become rich as individuals. They do feel vaguely guilty now. They have sinned, but they weren't punished. Something is wrong. (The guilt feelings of people who engage in sexual activity disapproved of by their puritanical tradition lead to a similar unrest.)

Jewish parents remember the past sufficiently to indulge, even to foster, albeit unconsciously, the radical attitudes of their children. At the least, the children become receptive to radical stimuli received elsewhere, if not directly at home. But quite often the parents keep the ideas and transmit the ideologies of their youth, even though these ideas may be out of touch with reality and with their own experience of it. These ideas are now irrelevant—to use a fashionable word—to the reality in which the bearers live, but emotionally necessary just because they do not fit reality, because they are now altruistic "ideals." They are used as opiates. Marx's own ideas of a future classless socialist Utopia often play the sedative role he assigned to the paradise of traditional religion. They function as a secular religion: they offer a secular "promised land." But the neo-Marxist "new left" ideas more often function as stimulants.

In one important respect, Jews resemble their anti-Semitic archfoes. Both keep attitudes and hold ideas and beliefs which are emotionally necessary to them. Both refuse to learn from reality and experience. Both get along in reality nevertheless. The anti-Semite may have Jewish friends. But in a corner of his mind, his general anti-Semitic prejudice lies untouched. His Jewish friends seem exceptions to him—generally Jews remain evil, greedy, etc.

The Jewish businessman gets along similarly. In his own experience, his success is not built on cheating and exploitation and treading on the poor, or on warmongering, or on any of the stereotyped devices to which the radicals attribute it. But he feels he is an exception. In a corner of his mind the Marxist stereotype continues undisturbed: capitalism is exploitation.

Many socialist countries are anti-Semitic and reactionary, and actually do exploit the masses and make life miserable, whereas Jews are free and unexploited in capitalist America. This, too, is somehow an exception and only temporary. In the end socialism must be better than capitalism—he learned so when he was a child. Therefore it is common sense. (Whatever one learns as a child is. What one learns later is, somehow, "theory.") His "capitalist" success does not change the attitude, nor do "socialist" disasters. On the contrary. He feels guilty enough about his success to support the dedicated socialism, the radical attitude of his son. After all, he can afford to.

His children now can afford the radicalism the father had to relinquish—at least as an active pursuit—to bring them up. The father became a liberal. He was once upon a time radical because he was poor. He felt he had nothing to lose, everything to gain. The children once more are radical—but this time because they are rich enough not to worry about earning money. Whereas the father's and grandfather's motive for radicalism was poverty and oppression, the marginal existence they were compelled to lead, the son's is a product of his parent's suburban success. The son discovers that "money isn't everything." It isn't. He is bored by money, by making it and by spending it.

Money shelters him materially; but for that he had to pay a price: he feels mentally uncomfortable, psychologically anxious, bored, restless, aimlessly rebellious—what is he to do with himself, with his life? His father's life does not appeal to him. He cannot see the importance of making money, or rising up into a higher class. He cannot see it precisely because his father did it for him: it has been done; therefore it is no longer important. In fact, money is not. He's always had it. And he cannot forgive his parents for regarding it as important, for devoting their life to making and spending money. He will not. He knows so much more than his parents. He does indeed—because he benefits from what they did and learned. Yet in giving them money, the father has robbed the children of the challenge which enabled him to live without becoming, or acting as, a radical.

He was too busy and too preoccupied to provide his children (or himself) with any other challenges. The need to make money and the effort required so absorbed the father's energies, so broke his back (as his son might put it), that he had no time to get bored, no need to become a radical to ward off the boredom. The son has. And does; radicalism is the only way to give a content, meaning, to his life.

The nineteenth-century German philosopher Arthur Schopenhauer found two major sources of human unhappiness: deprivation, which frustrates the poor; and surfeit, which bores the rich. The poor are stimulated and dissatisfied.* The rich are satisfied and unstimulated. The

---

* Unless they are so poor and so accustomed to it as to become apathetic.

121

poor wish for money; the rich for challenge. The newly rich are particularly bored, and those who are newly rich in a culture that offers few meaningful activities to the rich are most bored, simply because there is no tradition for a leisure class. So if making money is no longer "relevant," what do you do with your life? Making a revolution may become attractive: it keeps you occupied, it helps your self-image; and it seems more fulfilling to students than becoming a juvenile delinquent. In fact, revolutionary activity is the Jewish equivalent of juvenile delinquency.

In becoming a radical, the son also shows the father what he ought to have done. He ought to have remained the radical he was; he ought to have continued to wear the beard, the glasses, the European dress grandfather wore. The grandson makes up for the disloyal father who "sold out." He is going to change the system, and he is not going to spend any time just making money and allowing himself to be tempted to sell out as father did.

Is it true? or is it just make-believe? Well, the boys who do it think it is true. They have convinced themselves that they are the "resistance"; and by occupying the dean's office, talking groovy Mao talk, disrupting classes, reviving "Marxist dialectics" and the muckraking of the populists, protesting "imperialism," "exploitation," etc., they will make the revolution. The country is more prosperous than ever; income is growing higher and is steadily more equally distributed; "the working class" considers both Republicans and Democrats too leftist, and hates above all "the resistance." Still, "the revolution" has become an emotional need for the affluent suburban Jewish middle-class boys. Even if it amounts to not much more than a masquerade. Play-acting becomes a psychodrama and looks like reality. It is psychic reality—though no more, also no less.

The reluctant working class can be replaced. The Negroes are the new "proletarians." To them are attributed all the virtues proletarians used to have in the imagination of their would-be leaders—not least the revolutionary role. It matters little that, apart from a few enthusiasts and racketeers, Negroes don't like the role and won't play it. Proletarians did not either, but the radicals cast them anyway and went on rehearsing their own roles. The champions of the underdog need underdogs to champion. They have found Negroes, some willing to be championed, others not. But both will serve as stage props, and, hopefully, as battering rams.

Religion is hard to attack today—it plays no major role in "the establishment," or in defense of it. And it is often sympathetic to the rebels. Well, if religion no longer is the opiate of the people, opiate can become the religion of the people. Among the radicals and hippies, it bids fair to become just that. Drugs do perform some of the functions Marx attributed to religion: they serve as sedatives, as well as stimulants; either way they draw the drug-taker into fantasy and remove him from external reality.

But why so many Jews? What is specifically Jewish about radicalism? Further, are there no real complaints? no actual grievances? no realistic reasons for indignation and defiance? Of course there are. But, characteristically, the actual complaints merely rationalize the underlying need to defy the existing institutions, to paint those prominent in present society as monsters similar to Hitler or Stalin.

The old family memories of oppression are slow to fade

123

away. They have been internalized and are transmitted intact enough to be reenacted. Thus young Jewish radicals proclaim loudly and freely that they have no free speech—without even being aware of the paradox. The props may be missing, but the play must go on. The actors feel their acting is good enough to ignore the missing props and the incongruous scenery. They convince themselves. And, often, they have managed to convince college administrations and faculties.

We may distinguish among the newly affluent, newly radical Jewish generation several groups. There are first those who faithfully follow Daddy's footsteps—as Bettina Aptheker, daughter of the long-time Communist leader Herbert, does. This is easier to do for a daughter than for a son. A son often must compete and defy his father and become independent of him. How else can he be a man? If the father was merely liberal, the son often becomes radical. If their fathers were radical, they try to become *more* radical. As for the sons of conservative fathers, one meets very few, and they seldom are conservatives.

Of course this is too schematic. Some sons model themselves after their fathers and follow the paternal footsteps in their careers. Their rebellion is repressed or takes a different form. Perhaps they merely try to overtake and outdo their fathers in the same groove. But the scheme, if it does not fit all, fits most.

Those who have permissive, indulgent, undemandingly supportive fathers find it most difficult to rebel. They discover two expedients. They may elect not to defy the undefiable father, the father who is so permissive, so rational, so understanding and supportive; instead they defy a really bad father who does what the actual one never did: makes laws, rules, regulations—says they can't smoke pot, or prevent other students from being recruited for causes they disapprove of. These boys defy the university and the government *in loco parentis*. They protest the mistreatment of Negroes and Vietnamese, and in the process discharge all their anger; if necessary they provoke these institutions to act like the bad father who justifies their hatred. The institutions are first depicted as authoritarian and then forced to use police or close down so that the rebels can continue to play their role by successfully provoking the "oppression" they need to defy—and of which they didn't get enough at home to defy. In all this, the young suburbanites can identify with and may be supported by the good actual father who will agree with their grievances, pay for a lawyer, try to help with the draft board, and be proud of the son's defiance.

Those who wish to defy their actual fathers may have a hard time. How can you defy a man who does not stand up to be defied, who is always willing to help you and who is so reasonable it is hardly necessary to "sit in"? Can you accuse him of being nasty to Negroes? And how can you punish him? Whatever you do, he will support. These poor kids have only one way out. It won't do to be radicals. Daddy would just be proud of them. They have to become nothing. That—being nothing—is something they know he cannot support. So we have the Jewish hippies, who, though intelligent, refuse to study; though capable, refuse to work; though gentle, refuse to love anyone in favor of everyone, i.e., of no one. Flower children can manage to punish even the most indulgent parents by making a principle out of doing nothing and stultifying and destroying themselves. Theirs is a rebellion not against authority, but against the lack of meaningful authority.

But what of these parents? Where have they "gone wrong"? How did they drive their children to such extremes? Haven't they used the best and most modern methods? Haven't they given them everything, the best that money can buy?

The best that money can buy makes hippies and radicals both dislike money. For the best that money can buy is not good enough. These kids not only had the famed Jewish mothers—too often celebrated in song and story (and skit and caricature) to require depiction—they also had Jewish fathers. Fathers who gave the kids everything that money could buy, but were so busy earning the money with which to buy everything that the children were left to Mom, and ultimately themselves became the things that money could buy, the things that wore, displayed, and used the things Daddy could afford. Or so they felt. Something to be proud of, to show off with, to support, but not otherwise to shape, form, educate. That was left to Mom and the specialists.

The children have retaliated now, as hippies directly, or as radicals indirectly, by transferring their anger to public objects. They will not do what is expected, they will not enjoy what their parents prepare for them. They will, quite literally, spit at it. They will have contempt for all the material things they had in such abundance. They will care only for love—which they missed. (It might have been there; the point is they did not feel it. The parental permissiveness was felt as indifference.) And they will defy their parents by trying to overthrow the parental system—

the establishment—or by withdrawing from it, and meanwhile wear the clothes, the beards, the glasses, and the
unkempt look that Daddy left behind. They will be fla-
grantly "Jewish," an open reproach to their "American"
parents.

Is it serious? It is too pat to be. And the objective
American situation reduces it to no more than a passionately romantic gesture. But romantics have been known
to sacrifice their lives to romance. Sometimes they have
influenced events—though the outcome usually surprised
them. At times they have brought about needed reforms.
They may be wrong in their ideas, but their grievances are
felt, sometimes deeply, and some of the causes could be
corrected; the merit of calling attention to them is theirs.

The outcome may be different from their dreams. The
attacked institutions may even turn against their attackers,
who may find that they have, in fact, committed suicide.
Hitler and Stalin have been undesired results and reactions
to idealistic radical ideas. But the reaction in America is
likely to be milder; both hippies and radicals are likely to
become just part of the landscape. People will become used
to them and manage to take them into account as one does
a bumpy, slippery, or flooded road.

8

The Jewish Cultural Establishment

No LONGER altogether strangers to the Gentile tradition, no longer outside looking in, Jews now help develop and preserve and even dominate parts of that tradition. The effect is to revitalize, but also to change it.

Jews have developed a character and sensibility of their own, as does any group which shares experiences peculiar to it over a lengthy span. This naturally colors their outlook, focuses their perception, directs their expression, and forms their style. Homogeneity is not implied; yet the community of feeling, though elusive, is real—despite a dazzling range of differences from Goldwater * to Javits, orthodoxy to atheism, pornography to puritanism. Similar ranges of variation may be found among Germans or Italians. Yet we quite rightly speak of the *more teutonico* and of Italianate sensibility.

With Jews, however, the negative value that anti-Semites have attached to the words "Jews" and "Jewish" has been accepted by their friends as well as by their enemies, so that some of them in effect deny that the Jews are Jewish and maintain—as J. P. Sartre nearly does—that

* Jewish mainly (perhaps only) in name.

128

Jewishness has been invented by anti-Semites. "Ah, but you don't seem (look, act) *Jewish*," is the often heard phrase from well-meaning but condescending Gentiles who wish to flatter a Jewish friend by telling him he has none of the (nasty) qualities which the word "Jewish" connotes.

In the use and continuation of the Gentile tradition, Jewishness is a matter of style, of intonation, of emphasis and of neglect, of frequency and of prevalence—never a matter of total absence or exclusive presence. Given that Jews numerically prevail in some of our cultural institutions, and that in others they are represented in numbers and positions that automatically give them major influence, and given further that Jews have a Jewish sensibility, it follows that Jewish sensibility is likely to dominate some of our cultural institutions. It does.

Nothing better could have happened to some of the institutions so dominated. Of course, there is a price to pay —as there would be if these cultural institutions were dominated by the Irish (the Roman Catholic Church in the United States illustrates this all too well), by merchants, by proletarians or by Presbyterians.

American literary and political "highbrow" magazines offer the clearest example we have of this predominance. Here a bias, oddly enough quite unconscious, selects the subject matter, the treatment, and the authors most appealing to the Jewish sensibility (or which can best be fitted into it). It can be fairly said that these magazines are dominated by what may be called the Jewish cultural establishment.

The word "establishment" does not refer to a formal organization. There is no acknowledged hierarchy, visible or secret, no lines of authority fixed by explicit rules, no bureaucracy, regulations, instructions, or formalities. Above all, the establishment is not animated by a conscious common interest or purpose or even by deliberate hostility to outsiders. Often there are bitter attacks by members of the establishment against each other, usually in the pages of the magazines they dominate.

There is no conspiracy, and no organized effort of any kind to create one or to accomplish any specific purpose, be it only the increase of power. Yet the Jewish cultural establishment is alive and kicking. The various conspiracy-mongers know a half-truth only and, typically, have got hold of the wrong half. The establishment exists, though misperceived by outsiders, just as Jews exist. They, too, are misperceived, but they are not created by the imagination of anti-Semites; nor is the Jewish cultural establishment.

In any enterprise or group, some members, formally or informally, lead the others; they are more influential than the others and thus command more power. When these leading members have common backgrounds and have their hopes and fears directed to the same objects which help shape their characters, when they thus share attitudes and outlooks, they are likely to react similarly to many things: to approve or disapprove of the same persons, to stress (or ignore) the same range of activities. Affinity leads to understanding, and to the subliminal exclusion of those who do not share it, who do not speak the same language. A style of intellectual, moral, and esthetic evaluation is formed which tends to perpetuate itself by the selective perceptions and activities of the groups who generate it. They form an "establishment": a group of persons, powerful or influential in some matters, who share a range of criteria for acceptance or rejection of other persons and for the critical evaluation of their achievements and ideas. This is an unavoidable effect of a community of background and outlook. It requires no organization, no explicit understanding, certainly no common purpose. It involves common attitudes, shared emphases, perceptions, and expressions.*

People with a background and outlook substantially different from that of the establishment encounter formidable obstacles in being heard. Not that the establishment deliberately refuses to judge them fairly on their merits and to give them the chance they deserve; nor is there some conspiratorial purpose. Rather, the members do not easily grasp, let alone appreciate, experiences, backgrounds, attitudes, outlooks, personalities very different from their own. The merits of outsiders are not suppressed; they are simply not seen by establishment eyes trained to perceive things that establishment minds have been trained to understand. We do not understand how a Scotsman can bring himself to eat haggis; he cannot understand why we don't.

I once saw and heard William F. Buckley discuss on TV the prevalence of liberals in the communications media with—of all people—David Susskind. (The latter is certainly part of the Jewish communications establishment though not, I think, of the cultural one.) Susskind granted the prevalence but argued that it occurred because intelli-

---

* There is perhaps an economic parallel in the price leadership engaged in by some industries, where, induced by similar considerations and appraisals of cost and market factors, most firms change prices in the same way or follow each other without direct communication.

gent people were needed in TV—a questionable proposition
—and that the intelligent people just naturally are liberals.
People who are not liberals are stupid. (I am afraid Mr.
Susskind was serious: T. S. Eliot, Winston Churchill,
Charles de Gaulle, William Faulkner, and George San-
tayana are stupid in Mr. Susskind's view.) Apart from its
fatuousness, there is a logical error in Mr. Susskind's argument. He might just as well have said that the dearth of
Catholic scholars and scientists in the U.S. occurs simply
because intelligent persons are not Catholic; or that there
is a plethora of Negro prostitutes in New York because
Negro women are just naturally attracted to prostitution;
or that Negroes are rare among TV producers because Negroes are too stupid for TV.

Even if it be true that intelligent people are attracted to
liberalism, this is not to be explained by the virtues of that
ideology, but by the social and other conditions that cause
some people, stupid or intelligent, to prefer it. Personal
characteristics, including intelligence or stupidity, may play
some role but cannot explain the selection of ideology or
occupation or industry, because they may lead to many
other selections. People with the same personal characteristics—such as intelligence—are found on all sides.

The predominance of Jews in the communications industry—or in the garment industry—is mainly a matter
of historical and social conditions. In particular, for TV
jobs, connection with intelligence is most unlikely. It does
not explain why liberals get them, or why Negroes and conservatives somehow do not; such selections occur through
the sensibilities of those who dispose of the jobs, as is
always the case. Consequently, it does not do any harm to
be Jewish if you want to get such a job. Nor does it do

harm to be liberal; or, best, both. And, *mirabile dictu,* Jewish liberals are prominent in the communications industry. In fact, they dominate it.

The establishment usually confuses its specific sensibilities with general intelligence and aptitude. But such a confusion as that illustrated (but certainly not analyzed or even understood) by Mr. Susskind in this instance is itself to be explained; it is the problem, not the solution. The preponderance of Irishmen in the Roman Catholic hierarchy in the United States and the absence of Italians (or Puerto Ricans or Poles) is not explained by alleging that only Irishmen are good and intelligent Catholics (or that all good Catholics become Irish). It can be explained in terms of the history of the hierarchy and the factors that shaped its informal criteria of acceptability for newcomers. Any establishment acts this way, and the Jewish cultural one is no more an exception than is the Irish ecclesiastical one, or the Jewish communications establishment.

To Voltaire, the Gothic cathedrals of France were ugly and stupid—the very word "Gothic" became a term of disapproval in the eighteenth century. Often the sensibility of a period or place is not attuned to perceiving and understanding the values of another. To the eighteenth-century French, Shakespeare was a barbarian—and hardly anyone who is not French seems to appreciate Corneille and Racine. There is no gainsaying that the critical intelligence depends on the general background and outlook of its bearer, on his experience and on the sensibility shaped by it.

When cultural life is dominated by people with similar backgrounds and outlook and similarly trained sensibilities

133

—when there is indeed a cultural establishment—the limits of the range of taste tend to become more rigid; if the establishment endures long enough, the taste and sensibility that shape the establishment become the national taste and sensibility. Persons whose outlook and sensibility differ radically from what is current, or acceptable, within the establishment are unlikely to be understood by establishment members. They are automatically relegated beyond the pale. For them to be heard, published, read, understood, or appreciated according to their merits becomes very difficult.

"When I was a screen-writer for one of the major studios," says a former toiler in vineyards dominated by another Jewish cultural establishment, "we were talking in a script conference one day about how a mother would react to finding out her son had cheated in school. When it came my turn to speak, I said what I had to say. The head of the studio looked at me and said, 'Mr. O'Connor, no mother would react that way.' I told him that I had cheated in school, and that was exactly how my mother had reacted. There was an embarrassed silence for a moment, and then the studio head went on as if I hadn't spoken. My mother had slapped me around a little bit, and then sternly told me to go to the priest to ask God's forgiveness. The response they expected was that the mother would weep a little and take the poor, wounded boy to her breast. That's how they wrote it, and for a moment there, they made me feel as if my mother wasn't a member of the human race."

Once more, the obstacle in the path of nonmembers of the establishment is not a conspiracy to exclude them. It is simply a lack of understanding, often even a lack of perception that there is something to be understood. Non-members have the misfortune of being beyond the range of the dominant sensibility. Their merits are unseen. Establishment members, like people generally, recognize most easily what they have been trained to expect and to evaluate. Even when dimly perceived, the ability of outsiders is too uncomfortable to recognize. No one like to be forced to reexamine his whole outlook, the premises and precepts that have governed his conduct and his rationalization throughout his life—least of all when the articulation of these premises and precepts has been his life work and has gained him his intellectual and material position. This is what the admission of the outsider to the establishment, to recognition, position, power, and influence, would force upon the members.

Thus exclusion is a form of unconscious psychological economy or defense. It usually takes the form of a series of semiconscious minor but cumulative actions which never amount to a decision, never require critical examination, and yet have the effect of just such a decision. Each of the actions that result in exclusion may be taken for different overt motives.

What forms the community of background, attitude, and outlook that distinguishes the Jewish cultural establishment?

First there is the Jewish background. Often the parents were poor immigrants living in a Jewish ghetto—the children went to college, became teachers, literary critics, magazine editors, professors, writers. Sometimes the parents were orthodox Jews—the children secularized their faith and became orthodox socialists, maintaining the forms, the

135

tempo, the intellectual style, while changing the contents.

Sometimes the parents themselves already were socialists; often the children then became either liberals or communists. In the few instances where the parents already had advanced middle-class status, the children would start as liberals. The inherited and advanced outlook of the Jewish cultural establishment is certainly "left." Many of the members passed through socialist, communist, and Trotskyite phases but left these behind to remain vaguely and generally left, some still calling themselves, sentimentally, socialists; others, liberals. Out of this heritage comes a profound identification with the underdog, particularly the racial underdog. Psychologically and historically this identification is all too understandable; nevertheless, it is not morally justifiable.

To be an underdog is a matter of power, or rather the lack of it—not a matter of right or wrong. There is no reason why the weak cannot be as often and as easily wrong as the strong, and why the strong must be wrong whenever they fight with the weak. Weakness does not in itself yield moral superiority. Criminals are, one hopes, weaker than police, but are they morally superior? Few would *think* so, but many, particularly many Jews, *feel* so. The Jewish background produces a pro-underdog attitude —regardless of the rights and wrongs: Jews tend to be in favor of the arrested, not of the policeman who arrests him. They are concerned with the rights and needs of the accused, not with those of society; of the revolutionary, not of the *status quo* and its defenders. After all they have the experience of being arrested, not the experience of the arresting officer. There were no Jewish policemen in Russia, but there were many Jewish victims of arbitrary and brutal policemen.

The identification with the accused, the revolutionary, or the underdog prevails even when it is difficult intellectually or sentimentally because of their distance from Jewish attitudes. Often therefore the identification is topological rather than personal; the Jew identifies not with the accused, or the Negro, but with the situation of the accused or of the Negro. The situations and the people as defined by them, not the actual persons, are associated with persistent memories of the Jewish past.

Since the Jews suffered for so long from oppression by dominant groups, laws, and traditions, their sentimental identification with minorities, underdogs, the poor, the humiliated, the shunned, the maltreated, the outlawed is quite understandable. Yet, explanation is not justification. And unfortunately, the Jews have not used their intellectual powers to analyze Utopian, reformist, and revolutionary doctrines as effectively as they have used these powers to analyze traditions and ideologies supporting the *status quo*. Wherefore, within the Jewish cultural establishment, Jewishness as an entrance ticket has tended to be fused with vaguely leftist, pro-underdog attitudes. Jewishness alone merely gets you into the lobby.

Thus, Dwight Macdonald is fairly well accepted, though not Jewish, simply because he underwent the typical establishment experience and shares the establishment outlook. He was a Trotskyite, an anarchist, and has remained an unorganized, if not disorganized, leftist. His interests are literary and political—and he has always been with or defiantly for the underdog, whether or not it has bitten

137

him. He has a lively mind, a good heart, a brilliant style, and bad manners. He has been helped by all of these qualities.

Mary McCarthy has long been a member of the Jewish cultural establishment. She had impeccable credentials: a left and finally anti-Stalinist background; a brilliant literary style and mind. And an interest and concern with what interested and concerned the Jewish establishment. She did give it tone, as do Edmund Wilson and Robert Lowell, both accepted Gentiles, accepted because they share the concerns of the Jewish cultural establishment, its political and social attitude. It didn't do Mary McCarthy any harm that she turned out to have a Jewish grandmother. But it wasn't decisive, just as Senator Goldwater's Jewish grandparents and Jewish name were not decisive: Jews wouldn't vote for him, because he was conservative.

Affinity, not race, decides membership, but it so happens that the affinity is largely produced in a social group, a subculture, or race, which is Jewish. Those Jews who haven't got this affinity are out, whereas Gentiles who have enough of it (and other things to recommend them), can become part of it. But more Jews than Gentiles, proportionately, have the required affinity.

Irving Kristol is Jewish and has most of the required background (Marxist, Trotskyite, etc.). But Kristol's brilliant mind is now quite anti-utopian and leans toward conservatism. Once in the center of the Jewish establishment —as editor of *Commentary* and later of *Encounter*—now he is no longer part of the establishment. Even his wife —a distinguished historian—can't quite make it any more. Under her maiden name, Gertrude Himmelfarb, she wrote a pathbreaking book, *Victorian Minds*. The critic of the *New York Review of Books* (the journal of the Jewish intellectual new left establishment) grudgingly admitted that the book was brilliant; but he added that it was regrettably conservative owing to the seminal influence of the author's husband, Irving Kristol. Had she not married Mr. Kristol, the critic insinuated not too subtly, she would have been a marvelous historian. As it was . . . well, a nice try, but marred by that unfortunate marriage. (The critic was an English academician.)

Finally, Bill Buckley not only is not Jewish, but Irish and Catholic. Possibly it's OK not to be Jewish (although suspect). But to actively follow another religion . . . there are limits to tolerance. Moreover, unlike Irving Kristol, Buckley did not become conservative; he started that way! Finally, his father was an oil tycoon. Thus, although Buckley is no less able a writer than Macdonald, he doesn't have a chance. Both are Yale men, both are against the *status quo*. But Macdonald opposes from the left—and therefore is all right; whereas Buckley does so from the right—and therefore is all wrong: the traditional enemies of the Jews have come from the traditional right.

To the Jewish mind, the *Gestalt* of the rightist requires anti-Semitism. Hence Jews usually regard rightists as anti-Semites—no matter whether they are: they ought to be. Buckley must be evil, heartless if not stupid. How else . . . ? It matters little that Buckley actually is a rather sentimental fellow, more humanitarian in his personal attitudes than many of his political opponents. Nor does it matter that the disagreement between liberals and conservatives is not, after all, about or whether to have peace, freedom, and prosperity, but on how to achieve these goals. He *must* be heartless: after all, he is not Jewish and he *is* Irish *and* conservative.

It matters even less that Buckley is not anti-Semitic, or that a man by the name of Goldwater was a rightist, Buckley-supported candidate for President. Being a rightist, Goldwater, too, was suspected of anti-Semitism. Or, next best thing, a well-known Jewish pornographer took a poll of "psychologists" to prove that Goldwater was crazy (must be, to be so conservative). At the least, to be a rightist annuls one's Jewish credentials and excludes one from the establishment. To the pornographic-minded it makes one stupid, even crazy. Pornographers are, after all, specialists at stripping things down to the barest essentials.

The importance of the establishment—its power of inclusion and exclusion—is greatest where the criteria of competence are least objective, where leadership does not depend so much on objective accomplishments as on appeal to those already "in." Thus the establishment is of hardly any importance in the natural sciences. For instance, there are many excellent Jewish physicists: some are leftists; some are rightists; most are not very political. To be sure, rightists are less popular than leftists; Oppenheimer's leftist associations did not impair his popularity (as distinguished from official standing). Teller's rightist ones did impair his.* But in physics, being or not being a Jew has little effect on one's influence, one's power, the recognition

---

* Eugene Wigner's rightist stand impaired his popularity—even though he remains the only man ever to have won both the Nobel and the Fermi Prize. (All three physicists are Jewish.)

one gets, the promotions one may expect. The same holds in all the natural sciences.

In the social sciences, we find that being Jewish, but more importantly, being left, is of most importance in the least objective sciences, and of least importance in the most objective ones. Thus it is of little importance in economics. A "far right" economist—Milton Friedman—who happens to be Jewish, recently was elected president of the American Economic Association. I doubt that an equally competent, equally rightist sociologist could be elected President of the American Sociological Association.

However, when they do not display the right mixture of leftism and Jewishness, good economists will be altogether ignored by the Jewish literary establishment. The *New York Times* came very late to recognizing the outstanding economists around. *Commentary* or the *New York Review of Books* will ignore them in favor of unoriginal but liberal or leftist time-servers or journalists or of incompetents who repeat ancient sayings about the bosses or imperialism—things which are familiar.

The Jewish cultural establishment goes far beyond the strictly intellectual and academic milieu. It is spread throughout the communications industry and thereby enters almost every home in America.

Hollywood has always been a largely Jewish institution, pioneered by and founded by Jews. But L. B. Mayer was hardly a revolutionary. On the other hand, the television industry was founded and staffed by a much later generation of Jews. Both its cultural and its news offerings are

141

ardently liberal; David Susskind is not untypical either of the level or of the kind of liberalism spread. But it is not so much what is presented as what is left out in programming that manifests the power of the cultural establishment in the communications industry. Has one ever heard a balanced discussion of the situation in South Africa? Or a reasonable presentation of the "hawk" view on Vietnam? Or of the actions of a police force confronted with unruly crowds?

Once more, there rarely is conscious bias. It is what the producers are most sensitive to, and where their natural affinity lies. Wherefore when they plead innocent, they are sincere—they do not have *mens rea* (malicious intent), though there may be culpable negligence. In the main, they are biased because their background is such that they cannot understand that there is another side. Who could possible take seriously such *goyishe* views? The medium becomes biased because of the homogeneous background and, therefore, outlook of those who dominate it. (Of course they disagree among themselves. But family quarrels merely confirm familiarity. They compete—but for the same goals, and along the same lines.)

In some cases—especially on educational stations—it becomes hard to believe that the practice is wholly unconscious; and there is some indication that it is not. When compelled to, these stations establish "balanced coverage" by pairing intelligent and articulate liberals either with the most silly and extreme right-wingers they can find, or with a nice but befuddled administration spokesman. Senator Dirksen is certainly a fine man, but is it fair to offer him as a foil to Arthur Schlesinger? Of course there are more

able debaters, such as Sidney Hook, but educational television never seems to be able to reach him in time, nor
anyone else who could make an intelligent case against
the ritualistic liberalism characteristic of the Jewish cultural establishment. It helps little that Hook is Jewish, and
in his own way left. He certainly is not part of the
establishment. He's too rough on communists, student rebels,
etc. Why, he even supported American foreign policy at
times.

In as large and variegated an institution as *The New
York Times,* illustrations of objectivity and even conservatism can be found. But a liberal bias pervades the *Times'*
news, editorial, and even book review coverage. The bias
is not always as extreme as in the early coverage of the
Cuban revolution when, while the *Times* still insisted that
Castro was not a Communist, Fidel himself expressed his
surprise to learn as much. The total impact of the *Times* is
veering leftward from its former staid, conservative image.
Perhaps one cannot expect much else, for not only are a
good many of the reporters Jewish, but so are the readers.
And these readers are now of a newer and more leftist
generation. The *Times* has not led the new Jewish cultural
establishment, but it has now become a warm friend at
court.

Perhaps the best touchstone for discerning establishment
thinking are attitudes toward war and violence. These attitudes, which reflect Jewish feelings in intellectualized form,
are: war and violence—*against. Bitterly against* when the
enemy uses leftist symbols, or is, or represents himself
to be, an underdog. On the other hand, if the enemy uses
rightist symbols, or is a rightist dictator, or is anti-Semitic,

143

wars are just and necessary, and those who oppose them are obviously fascists or anti-Semites, or both. Similarly, leftist dictatorship: well, it was necessary to defeat the reactionaries, people really want it, look at the progress in education, housing (Cuba; North Vietnam; China, before it got too obviously nasty; Ghana under the redeemer). Whereas rightist dictatorships are just bad (Franco, Portugal, Taiwan, Greece) and remain so even if they are not dictatorships (Rhodesia, South Africa, South Vietnam). It is not the merits of the case that decide the issue, but the emotional reaction to rightist and leftist symbols, a reaction determined simply by the past historical conditioning of Jews as a group: the right tended to be traditionally, often extremely, anti-Semitic, the left anti-traditional and pro-Semitic. The feelings associated with the symbols now prevail over realities and often block perception.

Magazines important in the Jewish cultural establishment include *Commentary* (sponsored by the American Jewish Committee), one of the most important intellectual magazines in the country, edited by Norman Podhoretz. No other denominational magazine has achieved such intellectual influence. Articles are written mostly by Jews, but also by others; they are not restricted to Jewish themes, and are often quite excellent. *Commentary* reflects Jewish sensibility and intellect at their best—and is meant to do just that. What is remarkable is that this sensibility is no longer distinctive, but has become American sensibility.

The *New York Review of Books* (edited by Barbara Epstein and Robert Silvers), while clearly dominated by Jewish writers, also publishes essays by many English writers, thus trying, not very successfully, to take the edge off the charge of cliquishness. It excludes Jewish conservatives—the few there are—but includes non-Jewish leftists of all descriptions. The frequently first-rate literary articles have come to serve as a figleaf for "new left" politics.*

Partisan Review is edited by William Phillips and Philip Rahv (both Jewish, as are the editors of the other magazines). At one time dominating the Jewish cultural establishment, the magazine now is less important. It was, incidentally, this magazine that established the reputation of Susan Sontag, a perfervidly leftist lady, erudite, dull, and violently original. She is reputed to carry on a scandalously public affair with the *Zeitgeist*.

While on a lower intellectual rung than the preceding three publications, the *Village Voice,* under editor Dan Wolf, has developed such new writers as Jack Newfield and Richard Goldstein, who appear with more and more frequency in more widely circulated magazines.

Current writers who are given most attention by these publications are Norman Mailer, Saul Bellow, Bernard Malamud, Herbert Gold, Bruce Jay Friedman, Joseph Heller, and Philip Roth.

Non-Jewish writers of no less merit—John Updike, John Cheever, Muriel Spark, Donald Barthelme, to name a few —appear in the *New Yorker* magazine. They are highly regarded among at least some Jewish intellectuals too, but they do not belong—by tacit mutual understanding.

* The Jewish cultural establishment is now divided between old and new left factions. They are not on speaking terms. The old left feels that the United States is incomparably better than the totalitarian countries; and that it can be improved democratically; also that the United States is an indispensable bulwark against communist expansion. The new left, vaguely allied to student rebels, pacifists, Negro militants, et al., feels that the United States is the main villain in the world; that it needs a violent revolution; that totalitarianism is not and never really was the real issue. There are distinctions within each faction. The gulf between the two factions is steadily widening.

145

In addition, there are the numerous fellow-travelers of the establishment who are linked to it by shared ideas and attitudes, but don't quite make it, largely because of lack of intellectual sophistication. They find expression in the *New York Times Book Review,* the daily press, middlebrow magazines, and other media. (*The New Republic* and *The Nation* appeal mainly to academicians.)

It might be said, in the end, that a disproportionate number of books are bought by Jews and a disproportionate number of Gentiles do not buy books. No wonder that so many books also are written by and about Jews. This may help explain the dominance—certainly not the nature —of the Jewish cultural establishment in literature.

Jews are vastly overrepresented among musicians, too. Yet there is no specifically Jewish sensibility audible in the selection or performance of music, at least not to my ear. There is a similar overrepresentation on Broadway (and off Broadway) and in Hollywood; the effects are more visible than the effects of Jewish overrepresentation among musicians, but my competence in these subjects is too thin to discuss them fully here. I do not go to the movies very often, and I haven't been to the theater for years. Too often both media fail to amuse me. I have no doubt, on theoretical grounds, that Jewish sensibility has influenced what is being done in these media—just as would be the case were they prevalently staffed by Irishmen or Chinese.*

---

* Lack of space prevents discussion of the art world, where Jewish influence is considerable, symbolized by such names among critics Clement Greenberg and Harold Rosenberg, by prominent art dealers and experts and finally by some of the finest painters and sculptors. Here, as well as in architecture, Jews are prominent, but not as prevalent as they are in verbal and musical media.

9

Jews and Sex

THE JEWS have never accepted the Greek tradition of physical grace and beauty. Not only was that tradition alien; it was felt to be inconsistent with Jewish intellectual and moral values. Nor did the Jews ever accept the German cult of force, or the Roman cult of sex and cruelty. These ideals were irreconcilable with their own almost exclusively moral emphasis, though occasionally some Hellenistic ideas were at least temporarily fused with Judaic ones, ultimately to be repudiated in favor of the Jewish intellect and of Jewish ethics.

Yet the Jews never accepted the contempt of the body and its deliberate humiliation so characteristic of early Christianity; *De contemptu mundi* is not a treatise a Jew would have written. They could not afford contempt for a world to which they had to cling with all their strength, any more than a poor man can afford contempt for money.

Contempt for the body is probably a reaction to the conflict between bodily temptations and the Christian injunction to resist them. Jews think of the body as a more or less serviceable vehicle for their intellectual and moral

147

purposes. Like a horse, the body was to be kept fed and kept going—neither to become an end in itself, nor to be insulted and humiliated. In a sense, this attitude implies a deeper contempt for the physical body: it was not found worth insulting, depriving, castigating, any more than it was found worth exalting. After all, punishment of the body implies that the body is capable of very great sins and that it represents a major temptation. To the Jews, the body and its appetites were enough to be relegated among the unimportant things women were to take care of. The men could then devote themselves more fully to the Law—the one great serious matter in life.

The pragmatic and manipulative attitude toward the body has led to a certain joylessness. The body was deprived of its autonomy. It is not, as it is with Christians, in conflict with the spirit. But it is not in harmony with the intellect either. It is relegated to the position of a servant to whom one equitably gives his due, but who is not really part of the family, and is neither much of a threat nor very alluring. Frequently this Jewish attitude leads to polarizations, so that those involved think of their physical selves as perhaps repulsive yet necessary, and of their sexual activities as craved for and therefore to be gratified—to get rid of the nuisance, as it were (best by marriage), but never as something romantically longed for and fulfilling. One got married in obedience to law and custom, just as one would eat or dress. Singleness was frowned upon, and the Jews, unlike most other groups, never institutionalized it. Sex was engaged in almost ritually, at times set, if not by the Talmud, by custom of nearly talmudic standing.

Apart from intellectual exaltation, from the pleasure

taken in wit, argument, learning, intelligence, and wisdom, and in obeying God's commands, there was little prospect of pleasure for its own sake in Jewish life. Physical and even emotional life was more dutiful than joyful, more a matter of, at best, comfort than exhilaration. The biblical injunction against likenesses, which generated an esthetic repudiation of the body in art, and the self-exclusion of Jews from most strenuously physical activities may both have contributed to the shaping of this attitude. The body image may well have lost an esthetic dimension because no image of it could be made.*

Apart from procreation, sex was thought of as a dangerous disruptive force if not properly gratified. But *eros,* love as an esthetic exhilaration and as a romantic feeling, never made much of a dent on Jewish attitudes toward the body or toward the opposite sex. Love as a "sweet suffering" was too irrational. If you want her, get her. Longing for its own sake, as an end in itself, is, to this day, repudiated (why, it's masochistic!), and this repudiation is now regarded as healthy by most Americans. Like a river that is regulated to avoid floods or drying up, love and even sex, carefully and usefully regulated, lose their wild, spontaneous, impractical beauty—though there is an undeniable utilitarian gain; which is what occurred in the relations between the sexes among Jews.

Love as a moral quality, as *agape* or *caritas,* was never far from the Jewish spirit, indeed, always a prominent feature of it. And so was equity and consideration—justice

---

* The biblical injunction also may help explain why there was much craftsmanship but little art among the Jews before emancipation—a situation that has been reversed since.

and compassion. Sex was seen as a permissible gratification under legitimate circumstances, occasionally as a danger, but primarily as the practical vehicle for the perpetuation of the family line, and of the Chosen People as a whole. In this sense it became a duty. Thus, a widow was entitled by Law to demand that her brother-in-law marry her if her husband died before they had children, so as to continue "his brother's house."

Some of the individualistic Renaissance attitudes affected Jews in Italy and Spain who were in contact with them. And with emancipation, there were figures such as the highly romantic Heinrich Heine. But these were emancipated Jews. Unemancipated Jews even today are characterized by a nonesthetic utilitarian attitude toward the body, whether they are religious or not.

The historical alienation from the body and the rejection of love by utilization, subordination, legal or quasilegal regulation, and customary ritualization is apparent, for instance, in Alfred Kazin's somewhat cloying but obviously sincere description of his growing up in Jewish Brooklyn; * he notes that his immigrant parents felt duties toward each other and their offspring, and possibly affection, but regarded love as a goyish invention—perhaps an American luxury that their children might indulge in, provided it did not interfere with the serious business of life: education, success, and marriage. The children certainly reject this attitude consciously. But whether they succeed in excluding it from actual feeling or experience is a different matter—as anyone who has ever done research at Grossinger's will confirm. "Love is sweet," says a Yiddish

* A Walker in the City.

proverb, "but it's sweeter with bread." Erotic love and esthetic longings were luxuries which poor people, worried about their existence in the world and about God's approval of their practices and their observance of rituals, could ill afford.

Sex as a technical matter, yes; "love" as a moral matter, yes. But emotional passion? Not by accident did Spinoza, the most Jewish of philosophers and the most philosophical of Jews, write about it under the title *De humana servitute*—of human bondage. Even so, he not only disapproved, but also misdefined erotic love. He regarded love not as the human relationship it is, but simply as one's relationship to any external cause of whatever brings pleasure: *"quaedam laetitia concomitante causa externa."* This misses (or reverses) the point: it is love that causes the external event to yield pleasure. One does not love a girl because she yields pleasure. She pleases because one loves her. The gratification is an effect, not—except in infants—a cause of the love. And it is not just a simple "pleasure" that the lover experiences. It is love, not reducible to pleasure, or sex, or esteem, or respect, or any of the things to which love so often is reduced.*

The pragmatic attitude toward the body has many ramifications. Traditional Jewish women, for instance—most often in the extreme, unemancipated case—are sure that men do not admire their beauty, and they feel that they

---

* It is perhaps not accidental that the Jewish psychoanalyst Erich Fromm tends to define love in largely rational moral terms; whereas the Jewish psychoanalyst Wilhelm Reich came near to making love an orgiastic exercise. This polarization is part of the Jewish tradition, but alien to the non-Jewish tradition of love as esthetic longing. Cupids arrows were not aimed rationally.

cannot possibly be desired for their personalities, let alone their minds. They feel that men need them for relief, or service (among moderns this feeling is present as a fear). In the more emancipated circles they seem to utilize their bodies as instruments and promises—as means to achieve marriage or, in the still more emancipated case, as means for self-relief, peace of mind, and physical health. But love?

"Jewish girls are the world's most boring women," a friend of mine who is something of a Don Juan recently remarked to me. "They keep telling me that I'm not interested in their minds. They have a point. But when I tell them I'm interested in them as women, they burst into tears. Why don't they want to be women? Why do they want to be less than a woman? That's what a mind is, only part of a woman."

Fully emancipated Jewish girls will not confess to such feelings, nor admit them to themselves. But their self-image as instruments—even if it shines through only as a fear of being so used, as projection—seldom disappears altogether. And, under unfavorable circumstances, reality confirms it often enough. With this feeling, Jewish girls—urged on by their mothers—must get married as soon as possible. All forms of courtship which do not end in marriage are seen not as pleasures in themselves, but rather as exploitations, misuses: "she takes his money," or "he is just using her." It is dangerous to stick around and "play the market." Better have a secure thing—a doctor or a dentist, someone who can provide status and can provide for the children. Don't speculate.

Marriage, apart from a few ultra-orthodox groups, is no longer arranged by a *Schadchen,* the professional marriage broker who quite explicitly rated, bargained for, and exchanged all human qualities as if they were commodities which could be given an exact price. Marriage so arranged depended on the health and wealth of the girl, and the position and future of the groom—both largely evaluated by the families concerned—far more than on the attraction of the couple for each other, let alone love. The disappearance of the professional only meant that every Jewish mother has become an amateur marriage broker—and her daughter is involved in the bargaining even if she does not wish to be.

"Mom," says a girl in an old Jewish joke, annoyed because she feels her mother is not paying enough attention to her, "I'm going to put on my barbed-wire dress, paint my face blue, and go to the movies." "Fine, fine," says the distracted mother, "look your best, I understand the manager isn't married."

This description scarcely does justice to all Jewish girls and perhaps these days to a diminishing minority only. Certainly the attitude described is more openly admitted in the older generations than among the young "swingers." But it has its impact even on the latter, whether they follow the maternal lead or rebel against it. Courtship becomes a bargaining session. The man is to supply marriage, or in the case of the emancipated daughter, true appreciation of her personality (demonstrated by expenditure of time and money and, above all, "talk to me"). The girl in exchange will supply sexual relief, "take care of him," or subject him to the traditional ministrations of Jewish women: eat, eat.

The pragmatic, instrumental Jewish attitude toward the body has had interesting effects on the garment industry,

153

so largely dominated by Jews. From time immemorial, women, with the complicity of men, have tried to reshape and repackage their bodies so as to intensify the wish of men to open the package in the hope of being surprised by something new. Fashion always is ambivalent, seeming to hide parts of the body, actually directing the viewer's attention and curiosity exactly to what is newly concealed, or just bared. Men want to see what women want to hide if only to make men want to see it.

But some fashions are more than ambivalent. They hide and even distort the body—the better to hide it—under the pretext of making it more appealing. Brassieres can be used for this purpose. And girdles can serve no other. Both are produced largely by Jews. And both are utilized by Jewish women, who are famous for insisting on these items of clothing even when there is no functional need whatever; they feel respectable only when they are bound up, immobilized, and artificially shaped (distorted). Today among the young, there is a reaction in the opposite direction. Nobody except the foundation garment industry is sorry.

One of the great mysteries of Jewish life—to Jews and even more to non-Jews—is circumcision. "My covenant shall be in your flesh for an everlasting covenant," says God to Abraham in Genesis. He also says, "Every man child among you shall be circumcised." As a reward for keeping this covenant, Abraham is told, "thou shalt be a father of many nations."

To this day, even when they think themselves entirely "liberated" from all religious ideas or feelings, Jews will still have their sons circumcised on the eighth day after birth. (The significance of the eighth day is that it is the first day after the ritual number of seven.) If the child were not circumcised, he would be forever cut off from the Chosen People. He would not be considered a Jew by other Jews—no matter what the rest of the world might think. Even a Jew who feels on the whole that Jewishness is a burden hesitates to deny a son his birthright and his identity. "He can make up his own mind about religion when he grows up. But let's do this now."

The fact that loving parents would deliberately put a child through what is, after all, a form of mutilation seems baffling. Yet it is an almost universal custom, not only among Jews but also among Mohammedans and many African idolators (who perform the ceremony at puberty); circumcision is common also among the aborigines of Australia and Latin America.* Among both Jews and Mohammedans there is great pride in being among the elect; "uncircumcised dog" is a very serious insult in Islam.

Many theories have been put forward to explain the custom. Maimonides, the famous rabbinical scholar of the twelfth century, believed that God insisted on the circumcision of the Jews in order to reduce raging passions. "One of its objects," he wrote, "is to limit intercourse and to weaken the organ of generation as far as possible, and thus cause men to be moderate . . . the organ necessarily becomes weak when it loses blood and is deprived of its covering from the beginning."

Herodotus, in the fifth century B.C., said that the

---

* Circumcision now has become nearly universal in America—but for health reasons only and without religious significance.

Egyptians believed in circumcision because they preferred cleanliness to good looks. This same emphasis on hygiene is often noted by later Jewish writers who feel the Bible reflects sacred prescience about the lower incidence of carcinoma in the *glans penis* of circumcised males, less carcinoma of the cervix in their wives, and no phymosis. But it is unlikely that twentieth-century prophylaxis (or eighteenth-century reasoning) played a major role in archaic rituals. Anachronistic thinking of this sort—sometimes used as well to explain Jewish dietary laws—assumes that desert tribes followed scientific methods, and ignores the anthropological evidence which suggests magical and totemic beliefs underlying both the widespread dietary laws and the custom of circumcision.

According to Freud Moses, not really a Jew at all but an Egyptian, had introduced the Egyptian usage of circumcision among his Israelite followers; his purpose might have been to maintain their connection with the Egyptian culture they had left.

Originally circumcision may well have been part of the *rites de passage*—ceremonies in which the adolescents are taken into the community of adults, by marking them so as to differentiate them from the noninitiated.* The ceremony gives symbolic expression to certain universal fears and anxieties, and allays them at the same· time: circumcision among the Jews is an act of surgery which ends in a party. Few others do. Many peoples in the world have *rites de passage,* and many different forms of marking the child are used; often scars, tattoos, symbolic dress refer to the same anxieties, and become marks of tribal membership.

---

* Among South African Bantu-speaking tribes, upon circumcision the young man is told: "Now you are a man."

Some sexual anxiety is being dealt with through circumcision. (The Hebrew word for "bridegroom" comes from the same root as "to circumcise.") Perhaps the same magic is used which commands sacrifice of the first fruits of a field in order to preserve the rest of the crops from disaster wrought by the envious anger of the unpropitiated gods. (Possibly, human envy is projected upon the gods.) A part is ritually sacrificed for the whole so that the boy can grow up to be a bridegroom. "The mutilation of the genital," writes G. R. Scott in *Phallic Worship,* "appealed to the people as an eminently satisfactory means of offering a part of the body which would be most appreciated by the deity." And Abraham, whose name means "father of multitudes," was given that name by God only after, and as a result of, the circumcision covenant.

At least one god who is to be mollified by this symbolic castration is not as far away as heaven. The child's father is right there, at the ceremony.

The Jews are among the most patriarchal peoples on earth. They are the people who invented the religion of God the Father, and have refused for two millennia now to desert it for the religion of God the Son. They might well have a ceremony in which the sexuality of the son is symbolically sacrificed by (to?) the father.

Psychoanalysts maintain that the birth of a son arouses not only pride and love, but also anger and anxiety in the father at the intrusion of another male into his family. He must now share his woman and may fear to lose her. (Abraham, who accepted the covenant and its attendant circumcision rite, was also willing—with much protest— to sacrifice his son Isaac.) Deeper fears are aroused as well. The birth of a son also reawakens in the father the repressed, unconscious memories of his own infantile rivalry with *his* father. These feelings are projected upon the infant, as though the father were saying, "Oh, yes. I know what's on your mind. I used to feel like that myself." Circumcision may help to allay the unconscious anger of the father. "See," it says to him (in symbolic language) "don't be angry with him. He's little, he pays tribute to you and is in pain. Be compassionate and love him." The Bible suggests as much. Jehovah encountered Moses at an inn and sought to kill him. So Moses' wife took a flint and cut off the foreskin of her son, and cast it at Moses' feet; and she said: "Surely a bloody husband art thou to me." And the Bible continues: "So he let him go." * This is one of the more obscure passages in the Bible—probably parts of the story are missing. Interpreters disagree, but one thing seems clear. Someone was angry, and pacified only by "the blood of circumcision."

"If you miss a holy day," a Jew will tell you, "it comes around the next week, or the next year, and it's not too late to make it up. The same with a fault you might commit. You can atone for it, or make it good. But if you are not circumcised on the eighth day, it is too late for the rest of your life. That day will never come for you again. And it will never come for your children either, since you have broken the chain of tradition which binds you all the way back to Abraham."

Since every Jewish male is considered a member of the religious community, the ceremony according to tradition can be performed by any adult male. But the father was

* Exodus IV: 24-26.

preferred. However, in modern times, the function has come to be entrusted to a specially trained man. He is called a *mohel*. (In the United States a physician is often preferred to him.) The old flint knife of the Bible is no longer used; a double-edged steel knife is substituted. (A double-edge is specified, since it is felt that if the *mohel* should accidentally try to perform the operation with the dull side, the baby would be hurt. Usually, the *mohel* carries more than one knife, in case for some reason the first one should prove defective.)

The ceremony begins with the infant's godfather delivering him over for the operation. In Jewish tradition the godfather is usually an older man, and the most learned that can be found. He hands the little boy over to someone else, called the *sondek* (derived from the Greek *"syndikos"* meaning "representative"). The *sondek* holds the infant while the *mohel* performs the operation. The unconscious meaning here seems to be that the father, by interposing two other men between himself and the ceremony, is acting out a defense against the guilt he must feel for what is about to happen to the boy, and a defense as well against his own aggression.

However, the ceremony seems to have evolved over the centuries into a design which brings to the surface, and finally purges, the various conflicting and ambivalent emotions. The father's role cannot be denied after all: the *mohel* must turn to him and specifically ask him to state that he (the *mohel*) is acting solely as the agent for the father.

Then the entire congregation of people at the ceremony are brought in to share the guilt. "If this act is performed timidly," they must recite aloud and together, "or with soft heart, it is null and void." Here the recognition of universally shared but no less taboo emotions is used to keep them under (social) control. In primitive rites, where this hostility is directed not at an infant but at an adolescent, he is often beaten or made to run the gauntlet, or left in the jungle for days or nights to suffer alone, so as to prove himself worthy to join the community of adults who, by the ceremony, have discharged the hostility aroused by their young rivals.

The operation itself takes just a few seconds. The foreskin is quickly cut and removed from the *glans,* while the *mohel* recites this sentence: "O Living God, command to preserve our beloved flesh from destruction"—clear recognition that the sacrificed, dead piece of flesh is the price demanded to preserve the rest of the "beloved flesh."

Finally, the blood is stanched, in a highly symbolic manner. A venerable and honored guest is asked to apply his mouth to the penis, and suck up the first drop of blood. This is an essential step. Yet it is not often fully and specifically found in English versions of the original text. "The Compassionate One [God]," it reads in the original, "will bless him who circumcises the foreskin, and him who uncovers [the glans], and him who sucks up the blood of the circumcision." In the Standard American Prayerbook, this is translated as ". . . him who fulfills every part of the precept."

Here the rationalist, liberal and genteel spirit of later Judaism is at work. It rejects, and even refuses to acknowledge, the meaning of symbolic acts produced by unconscious impulses and fears. Thereby these acts are

160

deprived of much that made them emotionally significant. They are continued as a tradition, the meaning of which becomes more and more hidden to those who continue it. Or, a rational meaning acceptable to the modern mind is given, however anachronistic it may be, and the ceremony is muted and changed to conform to it. The whole matter is explained as a sanitary measure. Yet food taboos as well as circumcision practices were symbolic expressions of ideas and feelings about the world—in the case of Jews no less than in the case of contemporary African tribes.

Originally, then, circumcision meant that the revered and feared father accepted the blood sacrifice of the infant, and so accepted the child and allowed him to live. Simultaneously, circumcision involves ritual atonement on the part of the older man (acting for the father) for having drawn the blood of the infant, and an effort to heal (stanch) the wound. The blood is essential to the ceremony. If for some reason the child is born naturally circumcised, the *mohel* will nevertheless scratch him with the knife so as to draw a drop or two of blood.

Finally, the newly circumcised infant is blessed, and a happy celebration begins. "Even as he has entered into the Covenant," says the *mohel,* "so may he enter into the Torah, into the nuptial canopy and into good deeds."

"Entering into the Torah" means entering into the traditional male adult life of a Jew: study and learning; the "good deeds" mentioned sound like a further parental admonition against the wicked acts which circumcision is meant both to prevent and punish. And the stated permission granted the boy by his elders to "enter into the nuptial canopy" is what the whole ceremony has been about. Sex

161

and the body, having been sufficiently mutilated in semi-symbolic form, are now accepted and permitted. The father is reconciled to the son. The son has paid the price for the acceptance of his sex, and therewith he is accepted as a Jew also. His body itself has become a symbol of their covenant.

10

Do Jews Make Better Doctors?

SINCE at least the Middle Ages, Jews have been famed in the Western world for their skill as physicians. What led to this eminence? And what effects did it have?

The pragmatic Jewish attitude toward the body fostered a detached study of its physical workings. It led also to practical medical reasoning. Because it was not venerated esthetically, exploited sensually, or despised religiously, the Jewish body was kept in serviceable condition as an instrument helpful in the pursuit of the intellectual life—the ultimate purpose of Jewish existence. It could not be allowed to interfere.

Jews never believed in humiliating, depriving, or scourging the body. They did not welcome its sufferings but treated it as a servant who will serve better if treated fairly and provided for—but not spoiled.

In contrast, the tradition of Christian medieval medicine abounded with metaphysical ideas attached to various bodily functions and was distorted with superstition and fear. The body was regarded as the devil's instrument, as temptation incarnate, to be humiliated, made to suffer, and, at best, to be contemptuously neglected.

Dogmatic reliance on metaphysical authority made much of Christian medieval medicine more deadly than simple ignorance. Jewish physicians were not subject to that authority. Further, unlike their Christian colleagues, Jewish physicians had preserved—as had the Arabs—remnants of Hellenistic medical knowledge which Christian hostility to paganism had nearly extinguished elsewhere.

In addition, the Jewish religious tradition had developed a fairly detailed corpus of knowledge and of practices regarding the human body and its diseases. The almost obsessive Jewish concern that the food they ate be ritually "clean" rather than "unclean" played a role in this, as did the ritual slaughter of animals. The Talmud contains a great many anatomical observations on what constitutes a "clean," and thus edible animal, and by what signs a tainted animal (one which may have looked healthy, but had contracted a hidden disease) could be recognized. From this carefully built-up body of knowledge of disease in animals, the step to knowledge of disease in man could not have been very difficult.

The confidence many medieval princes placed in Jewish physicians was thus partly based on their greater skill. But the preference for Jewish physicians may have been strengthened as well by the superstitious awe in which Jews were sometimes held. They seemed strange and uncanny to Gentiles. The activities in which they engaged—such as banking—were unintelligible and seemed mysterious to many people (and are so regarded to this day by many). The very food they ate was different from the food most people ate. Perhaps they were allied with some supernatural power—demonic more likely than angelic, since they did not believe in the God everyone else believed in. Perhaps they did know potent secrets which helped them to survive everything the Christians did to eliminate them. Precisely because they were not bound by the restrictions that hedged Christian belief and conduct, might they not know more than good Christians could, or should, about the forbidden and demonic powers that might so easily gain possession of the body?

Unlike a Christian, a Jew allied with the devil did not risk losing the benefits of the redemption he had rejected anyway. So why not use the demonic powers that loss of his eternal soul may have won the Jew—without losing one's own soul? Such *arrière-pensées* may have played a role. And the comparatively greater ability of Jewish physicians, though flowing from altogether mundane sources, produced a therapeutic score good enough not to weaken the superstitious awe in which Jewish physicians were held.

If Jewish physicians were attractive to Gentile patients, Jews themselves had many reasons to be attracted to the medical profession. To begin with, medicine has the virtue of being highly portable. Medical knowledge, unlike wealth, was something even a Jew could not be robbed of. The Nazi persecutions have shown that this bit of medieval folk wisdom has not become obsolete. Unlike the German-Jewish lawyer, the German-Jewish physician did not have to learn his art anew when he came to America. The law differs from country to country, but the human physique responds to identical chemicals. Medicine, unlike most professions, is indispensable under any conceivable conditions and applicable everywhere. And medical knowledge yielded prestige in Gentile eyes—even to a Jew. Medicine does so in Jewish eyes, too, for this very reason, and also because it is regarded as a learned profession, and learning to this day commands overwhelming respect from Jews, be they religious or emancipated.

Physicians have universally high status. Rich and poor, communists and capitalists, anti-Semites and Jews, Protestants and Catholics—all need and respect physicians. In darkest Africa the medicine man is held in awe, as is the "headshrinker" in New York.

Medicine is one learned profession in which success does not depend on the approval of authority, but, to a much larger extent, on one's own demonstration of ability. Thus many of the attractions of medicine are analogous to the attractions of financial activity: it is universal, rational, independent of (often anti-Semitic) custom, everywhere useful, and not easily confiscated. In addition, there is respect for the physician and safety of income.

Which is, of course, the reason why "my son, the doctor" is traditionally every Jewish mother's dream, and "my son-in-law, the doctor" her greatest ambition for her daughter. To become a physician is the very symbol of upward movement in a secular society, yet it is one upward movement which also fits into the framework of traditional values. Thus "my son, the doctor" is a move up in secular and non-Jewish society—and a move up as well along the traditional Jewish lines. The physician is a professional, a learned man, almost like a rabbi—but unlike a rabbi nowadays, he has a steady income and is sought after by everyone, Jew and Gentile alike. He deals with "science" (or at least "facts"), which for Jews, as for Gentiles, is

166

taking the place formerly occupied by religion. Problems of marriage, sex, children, relatives, "human relations"— all subjects on which a rabbi or priest would have been consulted upon in the past—today are brought to the doctor.

The many famous Jewish physicians did not change the image of the Jew in the Gentile mind. Thus Jewish prominence in medicine, which has continued to this day, has not weakened the widespread belief that, unlike Gentiles, Jews do not care to work with their hands and are parasitic and unproductive.

Indeed, up to the nineteenth century in many places Jews were not allowed to perform manual labor, whether or not they cared for it. For example, Frederick the Great, who ruled Prussia from 1740 to 1786, decreed in 1756: "We herewith . . . order earnestly that in the future no Jew shall presume to engage in any manual trade." (Jews were allowed to engage in commercial and financial activity only. Yet so much of the work of the physician is manual: think of surgery, or obstetrics, for instance. Nevertheless, the image continues; it is not based on logic or fact, but on fear and desire.

Physicians, like lawyers, are dimly perceived as trying to get a reprieve for us, by means fair or foul, from the stern powers on which our fate depends: laws, natural and legal. They deal with arcane authorities above us, and they alone know how to work with them, how to bargain with them, perhaps how to bribe them, how to make them amenable to our wishes. We depend on these powers, familiar to physicians and lawyers, inscrutable to us. They may be implacable. But perhaps our lawyer, our doctor, may, this once, manage to placate them. Only they can spare us the punishment that otherwise may be inflicted for our misdeeds and abuses. In this sense, too, lawyers and physicians have split up among themselves the activities which in the Jewish past were practiced by the rabbis. And therewith they took some of the rabbi's status—and most of his income.

The ambivalence of patients toward their doctor is almost the same as the ambivalence felt toward Jews generally. The doctor represents both a threat and a promise. Your life depends on him; his skill and benevolence can save you, but he may also become the agent, or at least the emissary, of death. He can do forbidden things, explore dirty, dangerous, alluring and taboo regions of body and mind. To him there are no secrets, nor can you hide anything from him: *"nihil inultum remanebit."* He can cut you open and who knows . . . Certainly the image of the profession reflects whatever traces of sado-masochism are left in us. And yet the doctor is also a source of reassurance: he knows how to save us from pain and suffering; how to cheat death; how to keep us well. He can restore potency and life. The image is ambivalent—polarized in some people who need constant reassurance from doctors, and in others who avoid doctors at all costs.

To the layman, the doctor—hopefully the "good doctor"—becomes a father figure. Omnipotent, threatening, or reassuring—we depend on his power and are afraid of it. He may turn out to be the bad father who will punish us for our sins—though we hope he is the good father who will save us from them. Jews, as mentioned before, bear

168

the burden of being the fathers of our civilization, who imposed their moral values on our reluctant impulses. The Jewish doctor thus becomes a father figure because of both his origin and his profession, provoking negative and fearful feelings, as well as positive and hopeful feelings, just as a father might.

Can one ever have any but ambivalent feelings toward those to whom one entrusts one's life, and worse, toward those to whom one owes it—fathers and physicians?

11

Or More Aggressive Lawyers?

ACCORDING to the Bible, Abraham was willing to sacrifice his son Isaac when God commanded him to. God the Law must be obeyed, however contrary it may be to natural feeling. The Law, obedience to the divine sovereign, takes precedence not only over natural feeling but also over any individual wish, passion, fear, or argument, and must control it. Abraham followed God, not the objections of his conscience. It took Jews millennia to throw off the burden of the Law, to react and finally to overreact to Abraham's willingness to slaughter his son. They often lead now in "civil disobedience" to law. Meanwhile, however, their traditional obedience to law, reinforced throughout their history, preserved the Jews as an ethnic entity.

God also stayed Abraham's hand after he had tested his obedience. (The whole passage probably indicates the end of human sacrifices as part of service to the original tribal god.) Ever since, the Jews have fanatically insisted on the law, and have stayed its hand when somehow it became inhumane. They know how it feels to suffer both from law and from lawlessness.

When Jews lived in their own little communities (*Stetls*) throughout Eastern Europe, the rabbi was the highest civil authority of the community. In this capacity, one rabbi was asked to dismiss from his post a man whom the community found to be lazy and negligent. He asked witnesses to come forth. Many spoke against the minor official; only one man spoke for him. The rabbi dismissed the charges and ordered that the man be kept in his job. The people were dismayed. Why did the rabbi accept the favorable testimony of one man, when so many testified the other way? The rabbi replied with his version of the story.

"When Isaac was on the altar itself, and Abraham had the knife in his hand, didn't Abraham listen to the angel who came to stay his hand? And God found this just, though it went against His original command. The lesson to us is plain: To do a man harm requires a decision from high authority. To keep him from harm, a word even from one insignificant person should be enough." (The principle is reflected in the American jury system as well. A "guilty" verdict is not possible if a single juror refuses assent.)

Unlike the rabbi, I find it hard to see this principle in the Biblical story. However, chariness of majority views on guilt made more sense to Jews than to anyone else: they well knew who it is against whom the many voices are so often raised, and who can hope to be defended by, at most, a few.

Jewish attachment to law comes from two historical sources. Commitment to their own Jewish law and obedience to it kept the Jews Jewish: this law not only limited but minutely codified approved conduct; it shaped and suffused Jewish life. Gentile law, on the other hand, was the

171

major protection of the Jews against violence that arose from local hostility and superstition. The sovereign princes needed them; they perceived, however dimly, the usefulness of the Jews to themselves and to society. They protected them through law. Thus, Gentile law kept them alive —however precariously; Jewish law kept them Jewish. No wonder law means something special to Jews.

Their Law had to set Jews apart from the rest of the world if Judaism was to be preserved by an identifiable Jewish group. It had to impose onerous duties on them: nothing else creates and continues communal solidarity as well as meaningful common duties. It had to demand that they help each other far more than other groups needed to demand of their members, else it would have been impossible for them to work and live in a hostile world while remaining Jews. The ghetto (an Italian word of doubtful origin, most likely from *larghetto,* a little town or place) was at first a Jewish institution, an attempt at Jewish self-isolation, which, like many others, was later sanctioned and made compulsory and confining by the Gentiles. It was in the ghetto that the Jews could live a communal life and thus fulfill the Law. But the isolation could not be complete—it became necessary at once to obey and to fulfill, but as often to mitigate and to adapt, the Law to the circumstances in which Jews had to live and to make a living. Being of divine origin, Jewish law was unchangeable. Nonetheless, it had to be so interpreted as to permit Jewish survival: often survival depended on reinterpreting, if not altogether evading, the revered Law. Jewish leaders had to become adept at it. They did: casuistry was a talmudic tradition before it became a scholastic one.

The Gentile law protected the Jews, but under various pressures it often took with one hand what it gave with the other, by imposing tributes, duties, indignities, and limitations on its Jewish wards. Even England, untroubled by an Inquisitorial tradition, declared Jewish marriages invalid and bequests for Hebrew colleges void as late as the days of Pitt. No wonder the Jewish attitude toward Gentile law was ambivalent: the law was needed—it was protection—but it was precarious protection combined with oppression and discrimination. Though benefiting from the law, Jews cannot forget how they suffered from it. Thus, since emancipation, Jews have been cultivators, creators, and destroyers of the law. They are on the side of the law—but no less on the side of the offender. They display an ambivalent radicalism toward the law.

The attitude, in a way, is analogous to the Jewish attitude toward economic inequality. Wealthy Jews do their best to become wealthier, and poor Jews do their best to become wealthy. Both know that money is even better protection than the law, and both regard it as a mark of success—indeed, sometimes, as the very embodiment of it. Yet wealthy Jews have been known to support socialist causes; and their sons often are guilt-ridden about their parents' wealth. This, of course, happens in Gentile families as well. In a sense, it's only human. But a Jew always is more human or, to use the Yiddish word, more a *Mensch*— more radically so—than anyone else. The chasm between ideals and realities upset the prophets and never ceased to revolt their successors, from Karl Marx to Erich Fromm or Paul Goodman.

The long tradition of this ambivalence goes back to

173

the Bible. In modern times it reemerges at the beginnings of industrialization. For instance, Emile and Isaac Pereira and Olinde Rodrigues (together with other Jewish figures such as Léon Halévy and Félicien David) were quite prominent in the early French socialist movement led by Saint-Simon. Rodrigues and the Pereira brothers also became extremely wealthy, and influential in French economic life. On the one hand, their role in the Saint-Simonist movement spurred the anti-Semitism of Saint-Simon's rival, Fourier, and of his followers, let alone that of the French nobility and bourgeoisie; on the other hand, it fueled the belief in a Jewish conspiracy which indiscriminately prompted Jews to become leading capitalists and leading anti-capitalists: after all, both groups aimed at the destruction of the non-Jewish—in essence the pre-industrial—world, and thereby of those who were, or believed they had been, well off in it.

The actual explanation is simpler. Their rationalism as well as their sense of justice and their identification with the underdog (which for so long had been a Jewish dog), and not least their aversion to the *status quo ante,* to the pre-industrial era which had treated them badly, all led Jews to be less hindered by tradition, more inclined to innovation than Gentiles. We find a disproportionate number, therefore, among the promoters of new industries—who may become wealthy—and of new ideologies—who may raise the ire of those attached to things as they are or were. And sometimes the same Jews, though usually at different times, advocate a new social and legal order, and become wealthy by utilizing the old one. Or, finally, having become wealthy, pay tribute to their radical youth by supporting socialist movements.

Following Jewish tradition, wealthy Jews also give inordinate amounts of money to charity, philanthropy, and education. Their generosity toward education touched off a nationwide scandal in 1967, when a member of a New Jersey school board advised voters not to elect additional Jews for the reason that a Jewish plurality would raise the school budget and, therewith, taxes. He was accused of anti-Semitism—and reelected. I suspect that both he and the voters were mainly interested in keeping taxes down. It is true—and not at all anti-Semitic—to say that Jews are more generous with money for education than any other group.

Whether this is a reason for or against electing a Jew to a board of education depends on whether one wants more or less money spent on education. The connection with anti-Semitism, although superficially plausible, does not bear close scrutiny. Jews are, understandably enough, hypersensitive, sometimes seeing persecution where it does not exist, sometimes (as in Germany) denying it (or its true dimensions) to themselves where it is all too real. Whenever a man happens to be rejected for whatever reason, and also happens to be Jewish, anti-Semitic motives are suspected. Sometimes, too, the suspicion is exploited by self-interested Gentiles, for political reasons.

Such suspiciousness is not confined to Jews. Had Mr. Justice Fortas been a Negro, many Negroes would have suspected that his resignation from the United States Supreme Court was the result of an anti-Negro cabal. Of course, ethnic group membership can be an added motive for hostility; but if the group is Jewish, the hostility may be political and not racial. Jewish liberals are suspected of being more liberal than Gentile ones with equal credentials. The suspicion is based on the predominance of liberal-ism in the articulate Jewish community. And that predomi-nance is a fact. Seventeen per cent of Jews voted for Nixon in 1968 versus 49 per cent of Protestants.

Jews want to be wealthy, but cannot forget that they were poor so long. Though rich, they identify with poverty. Though powerful, they identify with oppression. And they assuage their guilt feelings: in the days before emancipation it was thought to be an act of great merit for a rich family to help support the highly trained, other-worldly youths who were devoting their lives to studying the Torah. Wealthy families on one day of the week would invite scholarly but poor young men to eat at their homes. In addition, the most intelligent and accomplished of these young men in the end would find they were in high demand as husbands for the daughters of these same rich people. Today, wealthy Jews do not marry their daughters to rabbinical students, being perhaps less other-worldly themselves. They endow universities instead, and are willing to tax themselves quite highly to support schools. Not surprisingly, people not as interested in education and those who suspect, sometimes rightly, that their offspring will not benefit as much from it as Jewish children will may resent the high tax rates.

One identifies with one's past more often—above all, more intensively and emotionally—than with the present. Although living in a society which does not oppress them, American Jews still tend to identify with those who are actually or putatively oppressed by, or in spite of, the law. This identification takes place regardless of merit; the cause of the underdog becomes the cause of justice. The past lives on to shape the present, or, at least, one's feelings about it.

Although they were allowed only recently to practice it in the Gentile world, Jews have always been attracted to the learned profession of the law. Their esteem for legal reasoning and judicial wisdom stems from Biblical times. Throughout the Middle Ages knowledge of the law was the main requirement for Jewish leadership. Legal training and legal reasoning were intensified by a history which made the law both the home of the Jews and the protection of that home. No wonder Jews are attracted by the law and excel in the practice of it; no wonder they are conspicuous in using the law in defense of the actually or putatively oppressed.

12

You Don't Have to Be Jewish Anymore to Charge Interest

FOR CENTURIES Jews were excluded by legislation from all occupations desirable to Gentiles. They were compelled to specialize in a few permitted activities which then became "typical." This helps explain the traditional Jewish concentration in such occupations as money-lending. It does not explain, however, the great number of Jews in the garment or in the movie industry, which may be due to later historical accidents, as is Chinese concentration in the laundry industry (in the United States) or the great number of Italians in construction or of Greeks in flower shops. The activities into which Jews were pushed turned out to be more important than many of those from which they were excluded for so long. Finance is one of them.

The exclusion of Jews in most places, and for most of the Middles Ages, by law and custom from primary activities such as farming was not the only cause which drew—and drove—them to money and to the financial and mercantile occupations most directly involved with it. Three other reasons played a major role.

1) Unlike Christians, Jews did not face religious prohibitions against lending money at interest.

2) The Jews were a homeless people long trained by their religion to deal with abstract ideas. They worshiped an abstract God of whom no images could be made, and who, unlike earlier and later gods, including His Son, was timeless and history-less, a pure universal idea. Money is a homeless, abstract commodity without particulars, a store and a standard of value, a medium of exchange and of account, an abstract, shapeless, and vicarious entity. No wonder money may be better understood by Jews and more congenial to them than to other people.

In the past, most people only occasionally dealt with money. Banks were mysterious institutions. No body understood why prices went up or down. Churchmen spoke of money and prices in moral (*pretium justum*) terms.* Speculation was abhorred, credit regarded as a plot to exploit or ruin the debtor. Yet money never was a respecter of traditions or of moral values. It always followed its own ways, beholden to none, with no loyalties except to unfathomable and abstract regularities. No wonder money was alien to much of the population. Yet this marginal entity was central to Jews who had to be—as few Gentiles were— merchants (and thus speculators) and money-lenders.

3) For centuries money also was the only form of power available to this dispersed and despised fraction of humanity and their only means of protection.

Each of these three reasons reinforces the others; together they go a long way toward explaining the position

---

* They still do. Churches as institutions have shown to this day more willingness to consider sex psychologically (as well as morally) than to consider money economically (as well as morally), despite such great economist-churchmen as Galiani or Malthus. To this day, churches tend to attribute low wages to nasty employers, and high prices to nasty merchants.

of Jews vis-à-vis money, even today. The association with money in turn helps to explain some of the prejudice against Jews.

To survive within a hostile society, the Jews had to be useful enough, at least to some powerful groups, to be protected from violence and annihilation. They could not survive by power of arms; they were only a small, weak fraction in any country in which they found themselves. They could not survive without some official help, or at least official neutrality, to prevent popular hostility from degenerating into slaughter. Through their ability to manipulate money, the Jews became useful, even indispensable, to the nobility, to princes, and to the Church itself. They became useful to these institutional leaders of the hostile masses for the very reason that generated the hostility of these masses— because they remained Jews.

As Jews they were outside the religious and social framework of the feudal system that dominated Europe for more than a thousand years. And just as a religious Jew, who is bound to perform no work on Saturday, will, if necessary, hire a Gentile to light a fire for him on the Sabbath, so the Jews were used by the Gentile medieval world to engage in forbidden, but necessary, monetary transactions. What to Christians was a sin was not sinful for Jews.

Then as now, people needed to borrow money, particularly those engaged in political enterprises such as wars, or those who owned estates or were engaged in building. Princes needed to borrow money for war and politics; the nobility often wanted to borrow on its estates, as did the

Church. Both engaged in a great deal of building. But who would lend money and take the risks involved while the loan was outstanding, only to lose whatever benefit he could have derived from the use of the money himself? Certainly nobody would if he could receive compensation for neither the risk nor the benefit foregone.

However, the Church for many centuries forbade Christians to receive compensation, to charge interest. Hence, only the Jews would lend money, for only they, exempt from this ecclesiastical prohibition, could accept payment for the use of their money: interest. (Paradoxically, one of the few fields of modern endeavor in which it is still widely believed that Jews are discriminated against is big-league banking. Historically Christians had a hard time competing with the well-entrenched Jews by the time they, too, could be bankers. They have remained chary of them.)

Laws against usury still prohibit "excessive" interest today. The idea that the price of money (interest) should be regulated by a moral norm rather than by demand and supply dies hard—even though we no longer attempt to regulate the price of cabbages or cars according to moral norms. "Excessive" interest is paid by people who cannot borrow at lower rates because they have little to offer the lender as security. The interest can be reduced by making loans at lower rates available to these people. But prohibiting "excessive" interest will simply make loans unavailable or, more likely, cause loans to be available clandestinely at rates of interest further increased by charges which cover the costs of illegality and of extra-legal enforcement of the lender's claims (the courts cannot be used to enforce claims generated by outlawed transactions). The anti-usury laws thus produce a living for gangsters and policemen at the expense of the borrowers, who presumably were to be favored. In the past such laws just helped provide a living for Jews.

It took many centuries for the Church to realize that you don't have to be Jewish to receive interest on money you lend. Until then the Jews were indispensable—particularly to those who were most able to protect them and who were also the main borrowers. This in turn reinforced the attraction that dealing in money had for Jews. It also diverted popular hostility from the rulers of the people to the Jews whom the rulers patronized. Bankers, even though "friendly," are hardly popular even now.

Jews also found it easier than Christians to form a financial community because talmudic law, unlike the Christian law of the Middle Ages, made it possible to transfer debts impersonally. Gentile law usually treated the obligation of the debtor to his creditor as a personal one. The money was owed to him who lent it, and to nobody else. Hence, the lender could not sell the evidence of debts owed him, nor use them to borrow for himself or to satisfy his creditors.

The Jews, on the other hand, treated debt as impersonal. The evidence of debt became negotiable paper. (The Italians soon adopted this practice, and indeed refined the techniques of banking even further.) The result was that a Jew could lend money and use the evidence of the debt owed him to borrow from another Jew who had capital available. Thus the Jews were able to form an international capital market. This was further facilitated by the contacts they maintained with each other, even though, or because, they were scattered in many countries. These contacts were based on their common religious heritage, on their similar social situation within the Christian world, and on their common culture. Finally, an international capital market was facilitated by the contacts the Jews maintained with each other as traders. Such contacts exceeded by far the mutual contacts of the feudal lords of different countries.

Perhaps the principal exclusion of the Jews from everyday life as it was lived in the Middle Ages was the prohibition against their owning land. In a world where wealth, prestige, and position were inextricably bound to land, this prohibition immediately put the Jews into an inferior social position. In addition, Jews could not become members of the guilds of craftsmen, which were highly organized in those centuries and guarded their privileges jealously. The result of such prohibitions forced the Jews to specialize in those occupations which, though indispensable to medieval Christianity, were for various reasons not regarded as respectable or even legitimate; these occupations, closed to Gentiles, were therefore preempted by Jews—and turned out to be among the most important post-medieval ones. The Jews who had been forced to devote themselves to money, to the exclusion of most other things, were prepared for the money economy that succeeded medieval feudalism. Those who had excluded them ended in part by resentfully excluding themselves from the money economy.

Fortunately for their survival, it so happened that the character of Jewish culture, derived from both the Mosaic religion and their actual social situation, prepared Jews quite well for the occupations in which they had to specialize.

183

The invisible God the Jews worshiped stood for a number of universal principles and promises to be redeemed—if the Law was obeyed. Money, too, is a universal principle, a symbol that can be redeemed at some future time, standing for the goods that can be bought with it. Its redemption, too, depends on observance of the law. Who could be more homeless or, to put it positively, more universal in the medieval world than the Jews? Who more than the Jews lived a life regulated by the Law derived from an invisible power? Nobody was more accustomed to abstract manipulation of legal and moral concepts —and hence prepared for the abstract calculations required by commerce and finance.

There is finally a set of psychosocial reasons drawing Jews to money and to the financial arts. Money is a form of power. It is the power to purchase whatever is sold. And few things are not for sale by someone. Above all, money for a long time was the only power available to Jews, who were politically impotent and could never hope for political power or for prestige in the Gentile environment. Money yielded what power they could obtain to protect them against their enemies. And what prestige they could hope for. And it is nondiscriminatory power. If "money talks," it talks to anyone, in a universal language regardless of tradition, nationality, or creed. And these—tradition, nationality, and creed—were the overwhelming foes of the Jews. Money, however, is calculable, rational, measurable international power, indifferent to tradition, and independent of the spontaneous power generated by emotions so often hostile to the Jews.

184

Finally, money, the universal power which purchases food, security, shelter, protection, and even respect, is a kind of power not easily captured or even grasped by any enemy. Unlike real estate or commodities, money can be easily transferred, moved, reassigned, thus eluding the clumsy pursuer and protecting the possessor. It was the only power available to Jews and also the power which could protect them most; the only material power that could be of use in their Jewish situation—namely, that of a people historically on the run.

With all or most of this understood by many people, one still finds an uneasiness among Jews and Gentiles alike about the Jews' traditional manipulation of money. Though it is known that the Jews were drawn and driven into the occupations of finance, they were not spared the reproach that they lived a parasitical existence. They ate, it was said (and not only by bigots), but did not cultivate the land. They had goods, but did not produce them. They were active, but their activity was not intelligible to the average Christian, and smacked of profiting from the ignorance or distress of others. To this day, many romantics feel uneasy about the Jews not being "productive," or directly "creative," but too often middlemen.

Karl Marx thought the Jews wickedly parasitic, scarcely pausing to point out that it was not altogether their fault that they were the pioneers of capitalism and engaged in some of its most characteristic activities. Yet the view that the Jews were parasitic because they were "middlemen" rests on a misconception, not of the Jews, but of the activity called "production" as contrasted with "trading," or "speculation," or other "middleman" activities.

This misconception was shared by many economists even before Marx. The founder of the French physiocratic school of economics, Quesnay, thought all real production to be agricultural; people not engaged in agriculture did not really "produce" value, useful as these people might be. Marx's idea about the production of value is analogous, though to him the "real" producers of values were the proletarians who were deprived of some of it (exploited by their employers): they did not get the "surplus value." Both Quesnay and Marx conceived of "value" as the product of manual workers—on farms or in industry—and thought of everybody else as a more or less useful "middleman."

Actually all workers are middlemen. Nobody "produces" in the romantic sense. Farmers do not produce milk —cows do. Farmers do not lay eggs—chickens do. Farmers are but the middlemen on the one hand between the cow and the fodder, and on the other, between the cow and the milk-drinkers—between the chicken and the chicken-feed, between the egg and the man at the breakfast table.

Industrial workers, too, do no more than to rearrange, to distribute, things in space, separating and recombining them. They assemble cars, or wheels, or put chemicals together, heat or cool them or dig them out of the earth— they do not "create"; they recombine, they separate and bring together.

And what do merchants and tradesmen do if not distribute things over space, separating and recombining them, or making things available to be combined, or bringing them to the consumer? Even speculators, by taking things

186

off the market when they are plentiful and cheap and re-
placing them on the market when they are scarce and dear,
distribute commodities more evenly over time—a very useful activity. Joseph, the first recorded speculator, worked
for Pharaoh and earned his gratitude. The Bible praises
him. But medieval scholastics, paying no heed, condemned
speculation as sinful—and left it to the Jews, without
honoring them as Pharaoh did Joseph.

The activity of the speculator, tradesman, or financier
is not manual but mental. Mental work of this kind makes
manual work useful and guides it—as does the work of
the engineer or manager.

Milk is useless unless brought to market in various
forms and in the right proportions. Automobiles had to be
invented. Production must be financed—and so does purchase. No need to go on. Anyone familiar with business
organization—whether under socialism or capitalism—
knows that the "middleman" is as indispensable and as
productive as the manual worker. The fact that distrust for
indirect, nonmanual work has survived so long merely
indicates how hard it is for most people to understand
production that does not involve visible, manual, physical
labor. How hard, therefore, to understand the Jew and his
invisible work.

Jews have always had the reputation of being wealthy
—quite undeserved on the average: a few extraordinary
wealthy and visible Jews tended to give credit to the theory,
or fantasy, even though most of Europe's Jews, far from
being wealthy, were miserably poor. Which was one rea-

son why they came to America. Where, indeed, they became, if not wealthy, prosperous, and clearly more so, and more rapidly so, than any other group of immigrants.

Although Jews were only 3.5 per cent of the population, William Atwood reported (*Look* magazine, 1955) that they received 10 per cent of the total personal income of the population; the disproportion was greatest in the highest brackets: about 20 per cent of American millionaires were Jewish. Although most Jews were far from being millionaires, they were better off than most non-Jews. Whereas less than 40 per cent of the population are classified as managers, professionals, officials, or proprietors, from 75 to 90 per cent of employed Jews are so classified. Nearly 15 per cent are professionals.

It might be noted that—as is the case with other groups —Jews are overrepresented in some industries, occupations, and firms and underrepresented in others. In banking— where Jews are underrepresented as they are in utilities and heavy industries—what Jews there are tend to be in "Jewish" houses. This is true even in merchandising (where Jews are overrepresented).

Such patterns do not necessarily involve deliberate favorable or unfavorable discrimination. They may simply reflect the historical attitudes and traditional selective preferences of employers or employees. Thus, Jews are underrepresented among the military and in politics but overrepresented among labor union officials.

High educational achievement undoubtedly contributed to high Jewish income, and given the motivation, the income helped to increase further the proportion of Jewish youth who attend college—some 62 per cent in 1955

188

versus only 26 per cent for the general population. (At present more than 42 per cent of the total college age population attends.) Obviously the general population still has a long way to go, whereas Jewish enrollment will soon be as near 100 per cent as it ever can get.

Chances are that the overrepresentation of Jews in some occupations and industries and the underrepresentation in others will diminish. You no longer have to enter the cloak-and-suit business just because your cousin Lenny will get you a job. Other jobs are open. And you do have a college education. However, the relative prosperity of Jews is likely to remain high. American income is likely to increase—but Jews are likely to maintain their relative position in its distribution: relative to their numbers, there is no indication that they will not remain the most prosperous of ethnic groups.

The Pecking Order Among American Jews, Then and Now

IN AMERICA the things that confer status change; so does the pecking order. In the Irish family, the cardinal's hat does not confer the prestige it once did. To the Jewish family even the prestige of the college the children are admitted to is becoming less important than it was. Today Brandeis might do. Curiously enough there is a return to the original status bases of the Jewish community, however indirect: descent, money, and career bring less prestige, intellectual and moral qualities more. The younger generation is establishing its own pecking order. It is different—though no worse—than the one before. As yet it is confined to people of college age, however; the older generation still largely clings to the old values.

The move from the lower East Side to the suburbs or even the upper West Side in New York—and there are equivalents in most big cities—used to be a move up. It certainly took money. And it inaugurated a more "American" style of living. To be sure, the environment remained Jewish—partly because the Jews wanted it so, partly because the Gentiles did. But it was Jewish-American, not Jewish-European. One arrived, as one had traveled, together with one's friends.

The younger generation has literally reoccupied the old sites. For instance, the lower East Side in New York is becoming the headquarters of Jewish Bohemia. To be sure, this move is likely to be temporary. Suburban living is here to stay, at least for the great majority. But the symbolic significance is clear. The children reject their parents' American-Jewish style in favor of the grandparents' European-Jewish style—or what they imagine it to have been. They want to reacquire the sense of community which the grandparents were supposed to have had and which the parents lost in the suburbs. So the young move back to the grandparents' old pads, dress in 1900 European styles, and discuss nineteenth-century European ideas as though they had just been invented.

They will learn, of course, that the past cannot be recaptured. Meanwhile they try. The new pecking order is romantic, giving high marks for rebelliousness, outrageousness, indifference to money and to official recognition. *Epater le bourgeois* is once more the order of the day— and *le bourgeois* loves it: *Hair* threatens to become the most successful musical in Broadway history. Nothing is more reassuring to the young than the belief that they can shock their elders. Nothing is more reassuring for the middle-aged than to show how much they are "with it" by declaring that, unlike others, they are not shocked. Not really.

This, too, is but a phase in the steadily changing

191

Jewish subculture. But an important one. "Our Crowd" is the past. These cats may be the future—if they are ever domesticated. So far they are not even housebroken.

As for the old pecking order, the distinction of having invented the word *kike* has generally been given to the German-descended Jews of New York. Toward the turn of the last century when the Jews of Eastern Europe, fleeing poverty, pogroms, and government persecutions, entered the United States in great numbers, the German Jews, who were already there, wanted to put as great a distance as possible between their own genteel, meticulously assimilated selves and these "foreigners." "Those Russians—all their names seem to end in *ki*"; hence "kikes."

Plausible as the derivation seems, Leo Rosten * has come up with another one that has convinced me. (He may even be right.) Rosten points out that the Eastern European Jews, though literate in Hebraic and sometimes Cyrillic letters, often were unfamiliar with the English alphabet and could not sign their names. They signed their immigration documents with a circle—the cross used by illiterate Gentile immigrants was anathema to them. The Yiddish word for "circle" is *kikel*. Hence, "kike." All of which by no means excludes the possibility that the derogatory connotation of "kike" has something to do with the German Jews.

German Jews went so far as to send a delegation to Washington to ask that the immigration of their co-religionists be slowed or stopped. And they assured each other that the East European Jews were "oriental," even of a differ-

* See his scholarly *The Joys of Yiddish*.

ent color. The poet Emma Lazarus, although herself descended from a Sephardic family, expressed the feelings of the German Jews when she wrote: "For the mass of semi-Orientals, Kabbalists, and Chassidim who constitute the vast majority of East European Israelites, some more practical measure . . . must be devised than their transportation to a state of society [the United States] utterly at variance with their . . . customs . . . and . . . beliefs." It did not worry her that there was a time when as much might have been said about other groups of Jews, including her own.

The *Hebrew Standard,* which thoroughly identified with the German-Jewish community, led by the great banking families of Seligman, Loeb, Schiff, et al., wrote that the German Jews "had no religious, social, or intellectual sympathies with [the Eastern European Jews]. . . . [They are] closer to Christian sentiment than to the Judaism of these miserable darkened Hebrews." If this sounds familiar, it just goes to show that Jews, however different, are not all that different: given the right conditions, they can be just as parochial, as anxious for their own status, and as intolerant and uncharitable as anyone else.

Before their own meteoric rise, the "Germans" reluctantly acknowledged a group of Jews a step above their own status—the Sephardim. They had arrived in America before the German group.

The year 1492, in which Columbus discovered America, was also the year in which Ferdinand and Isabella finally expelled the Jews from Spain. In the face of the Iberian persecution, many Jews were converted—some were directly compelled; others yielded to threats. (Several of these converted Jews sailed with Columbus.) The unconverted set off once more to search for a place to live as Jews. A large Spanish and Portuguese Jewish community was established in Holland; others went to Italy and even as far as Brazil. From this Brazilian Jewish community, twenty-three descendants of Iberian Jews eventually set sail for New York, or New Amsterdam, as it was then called. These twenty-three were the beginning of the Sephardic Jewish community in North America.

Since they were penniless as well as Jewish, Governor Peter Stuyvesant wanted to kick them out. But the West India Company in Amsterdam, which literally owned the colony, had major Jewish shareholders. Pressure was applied, and the Jews were allowed to stay.

The Sephardim, who thus formed the first Jewish community in America, are regarded and certainly regard themselves as the most aristocratic of Jews; at least those Sephardim who come from the Iberian peninsula. The African, Middle Eastern, and Asian Sephardim—particularly those who did not leave in time—are seldom regarded as aristocrats. They usually lived in a cultural backwater, were uneducated and often underprivileged.

Unlike other Jewish groups who grew away from their religion upon their arrival in America, the Sephardim immediately organized a classic Jewish community, with a synagogue, prayer, and rituals at its center. These Sephardim until expulsion had an unbroken history in Spain more often characterized by achievements in freedom than by oppression.

The American Sephardim were respected by Gentiles as

well as by the Jews who arrived later. Moses Lazarus, a Sephardic Jew, was sufficiently accepted to become a member of the Knickerbocker Club. His daughter Emma wrote the poem inscribed on the base of the Statue of Liberty. Her poem, which has America asking Europe to send her its "tired . . . poor . . . wretched refuse," caused a certain amount of muttering among the German Jews, some of whom felt that the "wretched refuse" referred to them, and indicated a somewhat patronizing attitude toward later immigrants. Emma herself apparently did not mean to go so far as to include "semi-Oriental . . . Chassidim" in her welcome to the New World.

When the "Germans" began to arrive in the United States, at first they joined the Sephardim. But in time, the Ashkenazim, as the German Jews and their descendants were called, grew to want religious communities of their own, annoyed perhaps by the Sephardic notions of their own superiority. The Ashkenazic ritual differed slightly from the Sephardic anyway, and there were many differences in community customs. In time, the Sephardim had come to be so entrenched in and assimilated to America that by the early 1800's some communities had begun to use English in their religious services, and the *chazzen,* the cantor who sings the service, came to be addressed as Reverend.

The superiority felt by the Sephardim toward the "Germans" was reproduced in the feelings of the German Ashkenazim toward the Ashkenazim of Eastern Europe who immigrated after them. They felt superior because of their earlier arrival in America, their consequent prosperity, and, above all, because of their established place in the community. The German Jews had arrived, as the Sephardim before them, poor and uneducated. Unlike the Sephardim, they found well-established co-religionists who were helpful to—if embarrassed by—them. The Sephardim acted as some people might toward a poor relative: helpful but from a distance. Now the German Jews acted in precisely the same way toward their Eastern European co-religionists.

The pattern is not limited to America: German Jews acted in a similar manner toward Eastern Jewish immigrants to Germany—until Hitler insisted that all Jews were *Untermenschen* anyway. And, of course, the pattern is not limited to Jews. The Puerto Ricans who arrived in the United States in the 1920's treated the later arrivals with contempt and were their principal exploiters.

Once in America, many Jews lost their religious beliefs and threw off the religious rules which had regulated their lives so minutely. In the old country, they all had been taught the practices of Judaism, but many knew little of its doctrines. The poorest and the least learned were propelled into emigrating first. As everyone else did in their old world community, they had observed the Jewish rituals. But in America, without a Jewish community to set, support, transmit, and enforce traditional custom, many slowly adopted the customs of their neighbors—though few ever lost their distinctive consciousness of themselves as Jews or gave up all tradition. As the waves of immigrants swelled to a flood, Jewish life was revitalized—albeit in secular form, in which synagogues became centers for women's clubs and humanitarian activities, and ceased to be centers of learning and of a life nearly coextensive with religion or, at least, dominated by religious rituals and suffused by religious spirit.

Although arriving "tired . . . poor . . . wretched," many German Jews made remarkable careers in America. Joseph Seligman, who was in time to become the confidant and banker of Ned Harriman, the railroad magnate, started as a peddler, as did many German-Jewish immigrants. He arrived in New York in 1837 by steerage; his entire fortune, the sum of $100, was sewn into his pants. Despite a promise to his intensely religious father that he would observe the dietary laws, Joseph had to break them as soon as he left home; the only meals served on board his boat contained pork. Joseph quickly learned the lesson that success in America, practically life itself, depends upon overlooking many of the old rules.

Seligman's career became a landmark in the history of the Jews in the United States. As he and his friends—most of whom began, as he did, as peddlers—grew wealthy, and wished to enter a larger society than their own German-Jewish one, they found their way barred by social anti-Semitism. Thus, when another Seligman tried to join the Union League Club, he was blackballed. The reason given was that, while the members felt no personal dislike for Mr. Seligman, they did have objections, which, it was made clear, were merely and "purely racial." This caused an outcry. The (non-Jewish) mayor of New York declared himself outraged. To show his support for Mr. Seligman, Mayor Gilroy borrowed the splendid Seligman coach, horses, and footmen to drive a visiting Spanish duke to City Hall; of course, he did not invite Mr. Seligman.

The reaction on the part of the German Jews could easily be predicted: they formed their own society. The "Harmonie Club" (which still continues, although in recent years it has allowed Eastern European Jews to enter) was a center of this society. The members felt themselves to be Germans of Jewish religion and descent, more sinned against than sinning. They spoke to each other in German rather than English, and cultivated their German heritage, Beethoven, and Goethe (Goethe, above all) rather than the Talmud. After all, they were not Chassidim, let alone Kabbalists, and they made this clear.

Just as the Sephardim had in time grown away from their initial clinging to ancient modes of religion, so did the Ashkenazim. Some of the great German-Jewish banking families grew so remote from their Jewish tradition that their children did not know they were Jews until they were old enough to leave home to go off to school. The news was broken to them, often in a quasi-ceremonial manner, as though it were a painful *rite de passage* which, once performed, need never be alluded to again. In one famous house, it is said that when a careless maid inadvertently let the fact of their Jewishness slip to two of the children, they burst into tears.

Of all the assimilationists, Joseph Seligman had perhaps the greatest passion for Americanization. He gave his sons names like DeWitt and George Washington, and most interesting of all, Alfred Lincoln Seligman; he may have thought, as Lincoln's father did not, that "Abraham" was too Hebraic.

It was also Mr. Seligman's idea to hire the author Horatio Alger to tutor his children; who could better indoctrinate them with the American way? (Incidentally, it was through Seligman's financial advice that Alger himself Horatio Alger-ed his way to fortune.) But the famous banker, who fought J. P. Morgan to a standstill in the Union

Pacific financial wars, would not go beyond a certain point in his eagerness to adapt to American usages. When approached by another member of his family with the proposal that they go all the way and change their name to one with a more Anglo-Saxon ring, Joseph Seligman replied that he himself was content with his name. He suggested, however, that if his relative wished to change his, perhaps a more appropriate name would be "Schlemiel" (fool). To Americanize is one thing, to give up one's Jewish identity another. Not only did Seligman not do so, but he would insist on his Jewishness as a matter of pride whenever it seemed challenged.*

When, toward the end of the nineteenth century, Eastern European Jews began to arrive in America in vast numbers, they came to a country in which the frontier was closing; the great westward expansion was on the wane. They tended therefore to concentrate in the cities, where jobs were available. German Jews promptly set up funds to be used in persuading Eastern European Jews to settle outside of New York City—as far away as possible. But the effort met with little success.

The German Jews found the Eastern Europeans to be, well—funny. They were socialists, anarchists, Zionists, radicals, all sorts of odd things, which the German Jews, as solid members of the middle class, could not help but suspect would disturb the peace of their drawing rooms. When they were not socially radical they were religiously orthodox and dressed peculiarly—almost as bad. Worst of all, many of the Easterners were also trade unionists; though

---

* Stephen Birmingham's *Our Crowd* contains a great deal of fascinating material on the German-Jewish families in America.

some had once been, like their German counterparts, shop-keepers, traders, or members of the middle class, they had become déclassé, proletarianized by systematic governmental anti-Semitism. To the well-to-do German Jews this reminder from the lower East Side was perhaps the most distasteful of all.

Nonetheless, the German Jews undertook the education of the Eastern Jews. If there was a patronizing sense of *noblesse oblige,* there was also a genuine sense of identification, and for better or for worse, there was a wry knowledge of being identified by others with their poor and unwanted relations.

The Eastern Europeans, in time, established themselves, prospered, grew wealthy, and, of course, set up societies and charities of their own. But they never ceased to regard their German predecessors with awe and some resentment. Charity is hard to forget. And sometimes harder to forgive.

In the years since World War II, the lines of demarcation between the various Jewish communities in the United States have tended to blur. But as late as 1950, when Robert Sarnoff, son of Brigadier General David Sarnoff, chairman of the board of RCA, married Felicia Warburg, some of the old German-Jewish families felt the daughter of their old friends had made something of a misalliance. Robert Sarnoff was hardly "poor" and "wretched." But he *was* a "Russian," wasn't he?

On the whole, snobbery has produced mostly comic effects among American Jews. Sometimes, however, the effects are serious.

In their social snobbery, a few Jews assimilated anti-

Semitism too; they identified with the hostility of the anti-Semitic environment and internalized it. Psychologically, this served to deny that they were themselves among the targets of the hostility. The identification with the anti-Semitic aggressor also made it possible to avoid standing up to him—an impossible task if one views him as overwhelmingly powerful and oneself as inadequate. Such an identification then permits channeling aggression toward a weaker target—those Jews who represent what one despises in oneself: one's own Jewishness, one's own Jewish origin, equated with inferiority owing to the internalized views of the environment.

Thus, the more assimilated—that is, the least Jewish— German Jews resented the "more Jewish" unassimilated newcomers from Eastern Europe who so embarrassingly reminded them of what they had left behind. American Jews resented and patronized the less assimilated, more recent immigrants.

This snobbery isn't restricted to America, by any means. Israeli Jews of European origin resent and snub oriental Jews. In short, the "emancipated," assimilated, Westernized Jewish groups resent those who remind them of stages of development, now surmounted, of their Eastern origins. While the content and the targets differ from group to group, the defense mechanism of identifying with an aggressor who seems too strong for counterattack remains the same. So does the defense of denying one's feeling of inadequacy by being hostile to those who seem to embody the inadequacy. Jewish anti-Semitism merely illustrates these universal mechanisms.

Although remnants of Jewish anti-Semitism persist in

America, they are much less prominent than in the past. The Nazi holocaust has reminded even the most assimilated that, in the eyes of Gentiles, each Jew is identified as a Jew with all other Jews, and may still be a victim.

Moreover, the Gentile environment in some Western countries, particularly in the United States, has become markedly hospitable to Jews. Jewishness is often admired and glamorized. It has become fashionable enough so that assimilated Jews have become nostalgic about their Jewishness, perhaps even proud of it, or at least more ambivalent where they had been negative. Psychologically, they can afford to. Jewishness has become part of a remote and distant past, a romantic memory rather than a present wound that hurts. Thus the assertion of Jewishness is more rhetorical than felt, and for that reason easier. The effect has been to free the orthodox and unassimilated Jewish minority of the scorn of gentilized Jews, and for some, to make them an object of respect.

Few American Jews would refer today to their more recently immigrated brethren as "kikes." Hitler may claim some credit for this, but it must be noted that the phenomenon—nostalgic return to long-left origins—is fairly general in America, though there are differences in the form it takes for each group. Negroes are becoming interested in their African heritage, and the Irish have long insisted on the greatness of their past, as have the Italians. But, as is so often the case, the matter takes a more extreme form in the Jews.

14

In Darkest Suburbia

SAYS ONE Jewish boy who was recently arrested (a Jewish boy arrested in the old days? Never!) for possessing marijuana: "Mom's all right, but she's always talking about the PTA and worrying about the wallpaper. You can't get interested in things like that. And Dad's all right, too—I can see that he tries to take an interest in me. He likes me to get good marks in school, for instance. But usually, he's too tired when he comes home at night for me to be able to talk, or do something with. He'll come home, very often after the rest of the family have eaten. Mom will have kept something hot for him. He eats, then he watches TV a while and falls asleep. It's the same with a lot of the other kids out here. During the day, we're the only men around! There's nobody to—oh, well—nobody to control us. We can run wild, and nobody notices. So we make up games, dangerous games. Like chicken. You have to prove you're a man, see? And one way of proving you're a man today is taking chances with the cops. Like smoking grass. My tough luck is only that I got busted."

Incidentally, since the father was not home when the

police phoned, it was the mother who had to go to the police station to arrange for bail for this boy. Jewish mothers dominate their families even more in the suburbs than they did in the city.

Suburban mothers have become dominant even in religion—the very province of Abraham, Moses, David, the Prophets, and the Lawgivers, and it used to be, of Pop himself. Only nobody would have dared call him that in those days.

"I never used to be religious when we lived in the city," says a suburban Jewish lawyer. "To tell you the truth, I'm still not. But when we moved out here, my wife said we had to affiliate with some temple—if only to give our kids a Sunday school to go to when they see their friends going. Also out here, well, joining a synagogue is a way of joining the community. You don't feel so much that you're a fish out of water."

"Who picked out the synagogue you joined?"

"My wife. There was a neighbor she immediately liked, and she asked her which one she belonged to. We joined that one. My wife likes it especially because they speak only English there. 'I'm Jewish,' she likes to say, 'but I'm not foreign. Why should I attend services where I don't understand the rabbi?' "

"Do you attend often?"

"Rarely. I bring too much work with me that I have to do over the weekend."

Here's what a suburban Jewish mother said in an interview: "I was raised in an orthodox family, and for the first years of my life, I never knew that anything else existed.

I outgrew that in time, of course, and so did my husband. He grew up in an orthodox family, too. I didn't think much about the whole subject while I was in college, but then I took a comparative religion course and it got me thinking about the subject again. Now that I'm married, and have children, I don't want to put them through all that heavy, old-fashioned orthodox business. This is the United States, after all—not Poland. But I do want them to remember that they are Jewish. So I asked my husband to relearn a few of the simple prayers—in Hebrew. Oh, just a few words you say before starting the meal, or drinking a glass of wine. He did, and the rabbi was helpful, of course. I myself have started lighting the Sabbath candles again—it takes only a few seconds. It's not very much, but it has made us what I want us to be: a Jewish family."

Some commentators have become concerned by the central role which women have taken over in Jewish religious life. The Jewish religion requires exact and specific detail. It has survived the centuries in part because of its almost obsessive concern for ritual, study, and ceremony. Yet very few women today care for the kind of life that this entails. And their religious education is not sufficiently sophisticated to teach them the importance of intense attention to detail. What results is a certain flattening out of religion, a blandness—just a prayer or two over the Sabbath candles will suffice to "continue the Jewish tradition." This, the critics point out, is not continuation—rather it is commemoration, perhaps nostalgia; something that is remembered, not kept alive, and certainly not lived.

On the other hand, while her husband sleeps in the suburban community and "lives" for his job in the city during the day, his wife does live in the suburb. She knows the community far better than her husband can or cares to. She knows its needs, the weaknesses of the school system, for instance, or of other areas of community action. She is thus in a commanding position to contribute to decisions in her synagogue and in the community-at-large for correcting evils and deficiencies. And since she is alone most of the day, with the children off at school, the suburban mother has formidable energies to put at the service of her synagogue's lady's club, or Hadassah. Her religion may be highly directed toward social ends, but her dedication and sincerity cannot be questioned. Yet the social results have become the ends, the religion the means. Religion has become instrumental in the suburbs and so has God, who serves as a heavenly psychiatrist bringing peace of mind.

Throw a bagel through the window of any commuter train heading for a predominantly Jewish suburb on a Friday night and ask the man it happens to hit why he is taking work home from the office to do over the weekend instead of going out to play golf. Ask his wife why her days are so frantically devoted to the PTA, the Women's Zionist Organization, the League of Women Voters, and campaigning for the March of Dimes.

The answer will be automatic. "Why, for the children, of course." "Nothing is too good for my kids," says one Jewish father. "I don't want them to go through what I did to get where I am. Sure I work hard. But when I think what this work will do for them, I'm glad to do it." "I want a better world for my children," a mother will say if you ask her why she is out ringing doorbells for an "idealistic" (i.e., left liberal) political candidate. (Gentile suburbanites often have similar attitudes. But as usual, the Jewish ones are more extreme.)

All too often these commendable attitudes result in the child growing up in an atmosphere where the happiness of the children (or of anyone else, for that matter) seems to depend upon the number of dollars spent to buy the trappings the parents regard as necessary to or, as symbols of, happiness—and these, the children rightly suspect, look quite identical to the trappings of the parental conception of success. The children themselves feel in danger of becoming part of that success, for the parents often regard the children as concrete manifestations and proofs of it—until they rebel.

"There were two houses on the market when we came up here looking for a place," says one suburban stockbroker. "One was going for fifty thousand, and they were asking seventy-two five for the other. We really couldn't quite afford the bigger one, but I saw that my wife would be happier in that one, so we took it. You only live once, you know."

It is hardly surprising that children soon pick up their parents' constant emphasis that the more expensive is the better—and from there to go, by an easy jump, to the conclusion that a lot of money is best of all. "They're always telling you that money can't buy happiness," says one suburban Jewish high school student. "They sing songs about it—the older generation that is—their kind of songs. 'The best things in life are free,' somebody like Bing Crosby sings. But I notice that neither my parents nor their friends act like they believe that. Nor do the slum kids in the city

207

act like they dig having 'plenty o' nuthin.' So who's kidding who?"

Another effect is that the children grow up in an atmosphere of nearly total permissiveness. "My husband and I spend a lot of time trying to make up our minds on how old our daughter should be when she goes out for her first date," says one young Hadassah member. "But all that went out the window when she came home and told us half her class had already started. We didn't want to come off like the kind of square parents you always hear about—even in our own eyes. And to deprive her might give her feelings of inferiority."

The parents might have added that they were concerned, too, to prove, as fast as possible, their daughter's popularity, which would reflect on her "adjustment" and, thereby, on the competence of her parents and on their success. Above all, in nonbusiness matters the parents feel too insecure to seriously assert their authority and insist on limits. They themselves are too new to the suburban style. They only know that the limits cannot be where they have been. The children often rebel against the lack of authority, although thinking they are defying authority, when the parents make a belated attempt to assert it. Above all, the children—unconsciously, to be sure—resent the parental permissiveness, which they perceive as lack of concern, as indifference.

An important moment comes when the son and/or daughter becomes old enough to drive a car. This is becoming a decisive moment in the life of many a suburban youngster. It means that for the first time in his life he need not depend upon his mother, who up to now had to agree to chauffeur him around or he didn't go. For a boy, in particular, it means that he can now date on his own for the first time and can act as a man.

"And yet the statistics on teen-age auto accidents have my wife and me scared to death," says a worried father. "If I had my way, my son would not be allowed to drive until he's twenty-one. But what can I do? I don't want to hold back my boy's social development. All his friends, kids his age, they're driving, too. Hell, they give courses in learning how to drive in the high school, getting the kids ready for the moment they hit minimum legal age.* How do you fight that? Now, my neighbor gave his son a car on his birthday, and the heat is on from my wife for me to give him a car. And I probably will. If they're all going to do it, I want my son to be among the first. I figure if I give in on this, he will not be in a rebellious mood when I talk to him about not drinking and driving, not going too fast, and all the other things my wife and I are worried about. If a boy is a social leader and well adjusted, and you've got his confidence, he's more likely to listen to reason. Isn't that right?" (It isn't. But to think so obviously makes daddy feel good.)

Some of the parents know. "I look around me and I don't recognize these children," says a suburban member of Mizrachi (this woman, significantly, is one generation older than most of the parents of whom we have been speaking, a grandmother). "Everything is done for them,

---

* Incidentally, the only known effect of these courses is to make the parents feel better. Insurance companies to the contrary notwithstanding, there is no evidence that high school courses in driving reduce accident frequency. Understandably, for such courses scarcely affect the emotions that cause adolescents to do risky things.

everything is served on a silver platter, 'the best of every-thing.' But they don't seem like Jewish children to me—even though many of them go to some kind of Jewish 'Sunday' school. They don't have any respect for anyone, even their parents. They seem like well-dressed hooligans to me. And not always well dressed. It's their parents' fault. They're just giving them too much—sometimes it's embar-rassing. They used to say a man showed off his money by putting a fur coat on his wife's back. Now they do it by having a catered party with music and a magician for kids eight years old. There was one in our neighborhood just last week."

The most recent development in the evolution of the Jewish suburban family is the hippies. Unlike the old idea of Jewish children as quiet, studious youngsters who never got into trouble with the law, the hippies are com-mitted to breaking or at least disregarding the law—yet they attract a disproportionate number of suburban Jewish boys and girls. And this disproportionate contingent of Jew-ish middle-class escapees also furnishes a great number of the leading spokesmen for the hippies. It is unavoidable that they be spokesmen—the Jewish group is the most ver-bal of all ethnic groups.

Yet, why are they hippies? One reason might be that to be a hippy is perhaps the only way left to the suburban Jewish middle-class child to protest against his parents' version of American values and ambitions—the suburban Jewish American way of life.

To be sure, Jewish middle-class kids were prominent in other protest movements. They sang folk songs, they demonstrated for civil rights. But folksinging left their parents neutral or nostalgic. And civil rights had their parents' enthusiastic approval, even if it often came from the sidelines and was flawed by the compromises men who make a living usually are willing to make in life.

To be a hippy, on the other hand, was guaranteed to upset one's parents, to worry them, and to make them angry. When every ambition may have parental support and monetary backing, ambitionlessness is the one way left of getting parents riled; it is hard to back one's hippy son's hippy ambitionlessness with money: he not only does not want to earn it, he does not even want to spend or have it. The parental support, even when explicitly requested, invalidates any rebellious gesture which would be shorn of its defiant (even if unconscious) meaning.

It is as though the suburban parent and the suburban school had conspired to drive the kids into becoming hippies. Whatever ways of rebelling they sought, parents and schools combined to support and thus to invalidate it. It is hard to defy one's parents when, as soon as one tries, the PTA asks the suburban high school to give courses in "right and wrong ways to defy your parents," and the school psychologist explains the whole matter to all and sundry. You cannot rebel with the support of the authority you are defying. The kids could find no target for rebellion; the authority was always supporting them. They had to defy everything—the whole system. To be a hippy is one way out, they found.

There are other reasons why the hippy syndrome—under whatever name—is a fit way to rebel, perhaps the only one. In a way, it is a retort. One may paraphrase it:

you have given me everything but the one thing I needed; you have given me everything money can buy—but not your time, your attention, your love. You have been indifferent to me as a person; you thought you could buy me off. (The parents may not actually have been indifferent. But the children feel them to be when the parents, alienated from their own individualities, were incapable of perceiving the children as individuals.)

Well, I am indifferent to you now. And I show you that I have no use for your money. You want me to be neat? I'll dress in the least neat way possible. You want me to use my brains for success? I'll use them to find new ways to fail; better yet, I'll anesthetize them with drugs. You pride yourself on being rational and on outwitting the world? I'll join a cult of irrationality and altruism. You wanted security for me? I'll live for the day. I will not be your American ideal—I will not be a clean-cut boy with a crew cut: I will be dirty and long-haired and messy and sissy and unappetizing. Nor will I be your Jewish ideal: I will not be a scholar, or a monetary success. I will be an ambitionless nothing. I will not even be a failure—for a failure is one who tries and does not make it. But if I tried, you would not let me fail.

Oedipal opposition to parental ideals can hardly go much further. It had to be as striking as this because "progressive" parents would not allow a natural desire for rebellion to be discharged against them—they would not be targets, they would not oppose their children. Society as a whole had to become the target.

The parental attitude of tolerance perceived as indifference by the children caused repudiation to take the form of indifference—the only valid response to parental indifference. Thus, for lack of intimate external targets, aggression had to be turned by the children against themselves: in the end, this turned out to be the only way of actually attacking one's parents, too. Perhaps it was appropriate. The main technique used by many of these parents to control their children was to make them feel guilty. (It is about the worst conceivable; your father is breaking his back for you and you. . . .) Now the children have finally retaliated; they have found a way of making the parents feel guilty.

213

15

The Sexual Power of the Stranger

As INTERPRETED and enforced by the rabbis, the Jewish religion has always made Gentile girls forbidden fruit. As such, quite tempting, of course. To most Jewish men, the phrase so often dropped from mother's lips, "nice Jewish girl," is redundant: all Jewish girls are "nice"—and thus uninteresting; Jewish men hope that somehow Gentile girls might be less "nice"—and more exciting.

Jews further believe that when it comes to sex, Gentile girls are more willing, more able, and above all more available. Of course: less like mother, less affecting perhaps, but therefore less inhibiting, more sexy. And because, after all, they are Gentiles, sex, pure physical sex without encumbrances, is a license one can take with them. They are the false idols, the golden calves around which one wants to dance the dances that angered Moses—so much more fun, precisely because they are not quite real; they can be idolized because they are not part of the family; and not being familiar, they do not breed contempt, or, at least, not boredom, so much more often the result of familiarity.

Philip Roth portrays the feelings of a Jewish boy, his hero (or antihero): "But the shikses ah, the shikses are something else again . . . the sight of their fresh cold blond hair spilling out of their kerchiefs and caps . . . I am ecstatic. How do they get so gorgeous, so healthy, so blond!" *

Throughout his description of Portnoy among the *shikses*—Gentile girls—Roth makes it clear that their attraction lies in the essential strangeness of their physique and of their mind and life style to the hero, who longs for what seems so different, so unintelligible, and (therefore) appears to be so free and healthy. The strangers always appear to be free from the oppressiveness of one's own tribal rules, from the possessiveness of the love of members of the tribe for each other, and from the cloying intimacy of too much mutual knowledge.

Gentiles have similar fantasies about Jews. Each group imagines that the other has the freedom to do what is forbidden at home, that the restrictions, frustrations, and demands imposed on one's own are not placed upon the members of the other group who, therefore, are free, like animals. Perceived as not quite human, they are held in contempt, but envied nonetheless, indeed more. The more distant the alien group, the more it becomes like a Rorschach ink blot invites the projection of the viewer's wishful and fearful fantasies about the things not allowed in this own group.

But there is more to it. Anthropologists distinguish exogamous tribes among primitives, tribes which permit marriage only to nonmembers, and endogamous tribes

* *Portnoy's Complaint,* p. 144.

which insist that members marry each other only. Exogamy is usually explained as the result of an extended incest taboo: the tribe considers itself a family descended from the same ancestors; thus marriage within would be incestuous. Endogamy is thought to display the other side of the attitude toward incest: the wish for it, and the desire to keep the identity of the tribe intact without diluting it with alien blood.

On the whole, it may be said that Jews show both traits. While even the marriage of cousins is frowned upon, the marriage of a Jewish boy to a Gentile girl is literally regarded by the traditionalists as a death in the family. Because they are outside the pale, gentile girls attract Jewish men. Forbidden normatively, morally, religiously, they become psychologically interesting; and they do not really count.

Sexual relations between Jews and Gentiles often have been marked by traces of ambivalence on both sides. To Gentile girls, Jews are powerfully threatening fathers—but also loving, close, providing, and supporting: for some they become the "bad," for others the "good" fathers. The power of this identification may have played a role in the case of a fatherless girl such as Marilyn Monroe, who converted to Judaism when she married Arthur Miller and took on Lee Strasberg as her substitute father.

Jewish family bonds are rather intense, and the feeling of Jewishness is equally so—be it accepted or repudiated. To the Jewish man, the Gentile girl not only has the attractions, the dangers, and the guilt-provoking characteristics of forbiddenness, but also the advantage of not burdening him with the intensity, the demands, and the foreseen obliga-

216

tions he associates with Jewish girls.

"Whenever I go to a party," said a Jewish friend of mine, "I never look at the Jewish girls, I know they're going to hold out for the wedding ring. At least, I'll feel guilty for not offering it. On the other hand, when I finally get married, I'll probably marry a Jewish girl after all— which explains why I keep putting it off. Jewish girls immediately want to make a home for you. But I still don't want a home made for me . . . just a bed."

To some extent, this phenomenon is general: the sexual attractiveness of the stranger is based in part on his seeming to be free, and freely available, unencumbered by restraints, relationships, and demands which arise from participation in the community. Because she (or he) is not part of the tribe, he (or she) is forbidden. But the forbidden person is sexually more available because he (or she) can be had without assuming obligations to the family and the community which are involved if one wants a member of one's own tribe. Because, further, he (or she) is not part of the tribe, there is less need for respect, and thus more possibility —at least in fantasy—to do things that could not be done with a person one has to respect. (In *Portnoy's Complaint* that is precisely the role Gentile girls play in the life of the Jewish hero.)

There is less identification with the stranger. He (or she) can be treated as a fantasy object. Many people never fully lose a feeling that sex (particularly those variations not accepted as "normal" in the group) is enjoyable but dirty—improper, not quite right, perverse, disrespectful, and punishable. For most persons (not, by any means, for all) the prohibition is lifted under socially approved circumstances, such as marriage. But the permission is limited; and the permitted activity, with the permitted partner, may become boring. For some, sexual enjoyment remains associated with impropriety—that is, sex is enjoyable for them only when improper or with a stranger, whom one can treat improperly, at least temporarily, as an object.

"When I was in the army," says one Jewish man, "we'd get a pass and go into town, looking for girls. None of my buddies were Jews, but that never mattered except when it came to women. If one of the guys would come back to camp on Sunday night and say he'd made it with a Jewish girl, I'd feel like hitting him. I'd feel as if he were somehow attacking me, making me feel cheap. I told this to my closest friend one time, Sergeant Clausen. I had a hell of a time getting it out, but when I did, he only laughed at me. 'Hell,' he said, 'do I get insulted every time you screw a Christian girl?' And he was right. Why should I feel that way?"

The identification of all women in the tribe with mothers or sisters (or, for women: fathers or brothers) may produce both a wish to protect them against the sexuality of others (and oneself against dishonor) and an incest taboo: one must respect them and not desire them sexually. This taboo is not as easily mobilized by a stranger, who arouses fewer of the fears attached to one's original incestuous desires. And, of course, sex with a stranger is less binding— more sex, and less obligation than is incurred by sexual ties to members of one's own tribe, or class, or community.

One factor in the attractiveness of Jewish men to Christian women is quite analogous. Yet although as strangers Jews mobilize incest fears less than a member of one's own group would, they possibly satisfy the incestuous wish of Gentile girls more. For in quite general sense, Jews are father figures to the Gentile world.

It may be objected that the causes listed for the mutual attraction of Gentiles and Jews are quite contradictory. They are. This does not indicate anything wrong, however. In the first place, one or the other cause, but not necessarily all, may be prominent in any particular person. More important, even in the same person, several causes which in logic are mutually exclusive may coexist on different psychological levels. If human character were consistent, psychoanalysts would be unemployed. The unconscious knows no logic. The conscious portion of the mind, which does, usually rejects and represses the part of the unconscious which contradicts conscious desires, or ideas. Our actions and, more often, our feelings are the effect of many, sometimes contradictory, unconscious causes.

In the past, though there were (more or less clandestine) sexual relations between Jews and Gentiles, marriages were rare. To the Gentile, there was a considerable disadvantage in marrying a Jew—it meant sharing the many disadvantages of being a Jew in a Gentile world.

"I'll tell you one thing frankly," says a pretty Gentile girl from a socially prominent family who surprised everyone, including herself, by marrying a Jew, "the idea of marrying a Jew never occurred to me. Then I met Robert, and I wanted to marry him. But I had to think about it for a long time, and even then, we only got married when he agreed with me that there was no reason for our children to be brought up to be Jewish. He's not religious at all—so why make our children carry the burden of being a member of a minority? I would never insult Robert by asking him to deny he's Jewish, or to come to church with me and the children (though he occasionally does, just to be fatherly), but I would never allow my children to be burdened either with a faith their father himself does not care about."

To a Jew, marrying a Gentile meant to be looked upon askance by other Jews while not being fully accepted by the Gentile world. Exceptions occurred, particularly in the American West. The few Jews there belonged to just one of the many pioneering groups. But these were exceptions, and the Jews involved usually lost their · Jewish identity, keeping, at most, the name, as Senator Goldwater did.

Intermarriage now is becoming more frequent, even outside the West, though still opposed by Jewish authorities. Oddly enough, intermarriage is opposed even by those "reform" religious authorities who have for so long proclaimed that Judaism is not a tribal but a universal religion, and that Jews are not a national but only a religious group. A very rational attitude, indeed—in fact, so rational that it now threatens to eliminate Judaism as a distinct religion, as well as a nationality. Religions are not rational systems, but historical creations which theologians attempt, with doubtful success, to justify by reason. And nationalities are certainly not rational creations either, any more than, say, families. In the Jewish case the two nonrational historical products—nationality and religion—which grew together, and shaped each other, seem very hard to separate without fatal damage.

220

The reasons for the increase of contacts and, as a result, of sex and finally intermarriage between Jew and Gentile are obvious. Jews participate more fully in non-Jewish social life. They go to high schools and colleges with non-Jews; they work side by side with Christians. They are politically and, finally, socially active together with Gentiles. Contacts have greatly multiplied, with consequent greater chances for acquaintance, liking, and love.

"Your generation is the one that's hung-up about these things," said a sixteen-year-old editor of a suburban high school newspaper to a TV panel moderator in a recent discussion about prejudice. "I'm Jewish, and some of my friends aren't, but we don't take these things seriously. Not my generation. It's only when we get around people like you, or these discussions you hold, or get into arguments with our parents, that it comes up. With us, we never think about it."

Even if there is a tinge of wish-fulfillment in this speech, it does point to the direction of modern American life—and the probable disappearance of the Jews as an identifiable group.

Love in America is accepted as true love when it leads to marriage. It is not treated, as it still is frequently in Europe, as a thing apart from marriage. On the contrary, marriage is felt to climax, to certify, and to perpetuate true love. Relations that do not lead to marriage are regarded as sinful if they never were meant to end in that holy estate, and as mistakes if they do not lead to it, even though meant to.

The Gentile is still alien enough to attract the Jew and vice versa. But no longer quite so alien as to be ineligible except for affairs. Marriage has become possible. In a way, this reduces the mutual attraction. It can no longer be a fancy-free affair, a weekend's passion protected against any thought of the future—and in a sense, against reality—by the shared knowledge that it will never be more and, therefore, never less than love (or sex, as the case may be).

Now it can also be marriage. That means that those involved can no longer keep reality out altogether—they no longer can see only the image of the other which each forms in his own mind, generated by wishes as much as by perceptions. Jew and Gentile have actually to learn to see each other as they are—to the extent to which this is humanly possible and, at times, perhaps beyond the point where each remains desirable to the other. Of course, the possibility of permanence also adds to the mutual attraction, at least of those who are both realistic and marriage-minded.

Their remain enough obstacles to such marriages to make them more romantic than others. "We were stupid to tell her she couldn't go out with him," says a rueful parent of a Gentile girl who married a Jewish boy. "She was bound to defy us, and since we brought her up as a nice, middle-class girl, she didn't know any other way to defy us but to marry him."

While perhaps romantic, or proudly defiant (and certainly sexually charged) to the young participants, intermarriage still remains difficult for the older generation. Gentile parents look askance at the idea of having grandchildren so dissimilar from themselves, who, perhaps, cannot even be taken to church on Sundays. The Jewish parents threaten to commit suicide, or, the next best thing, to disinherit their son. What does a grandson avail if he is not Jewish? He can't even say *Kaddish*—the prayer for the dead. And if the grandson becomes Jewish, is he really? when his mother, converted or not, is, after all, a *shiksa?*

If you can't beat them, join them. But who is joining whom? It is hard to say. It is clear though that as American Jews continue to win the freedom and the ease for which they have fought so long, as they continue to lose that stubborn, inconvenient, unassimilable, passionate core of purely religious belief which has been their bane and their blessing—as they become, in a word, more like everyone else—the rate of their disappearance will accelerate. They are dying out because of their own worldly success.

Even if one does not believe in miracles, the survival of the Jews seems like one. Abraham asked God to save a city if he could find as few as ten righteous men there: the quality of Jewish life is based on morals and belief, and not on numbers. It may be that the prophet Isaiah will be vindicated when "In those days ten men from the nations of every tongue shall take hold of the robe of a Jew, saying, 'Let us go with you, for we have heard that God is with you.' " Will there be enough Jews left to go around?

16

The Vanishing Jew

IF PRESENT trends continue, in the year 2000 there will have never been more handsome, better-endowed synagogues in America, nor so many; nor so few Jews. The prediction of David Ben Gurion, Israel's former Prime Minister, that American Jewry is a dying branch may come true. Why has this happened in the country which has been for Jews the promised land of milk and honey more than any other?

For millennia Jews intermarried less than any other group. Sexual ghettoization went hand-in-hand with geographic ghettoization and was thought a good idea on both sides: if the rest of the population did not want Jews to leave their enclaves for fear of contamination, unpleasantness, and pollution, the Jews, on their part, did not want outsiders to enter for fear of contamination, unpleasantness, and pollution. And people usually marry their neighbors; the more so the fewer the other families they know.

As for intermarriage, the contempt of many Jews for the *goy* was matched only by the contempt of many Gentiles for the Jew. And then there was religion. If a son brought home a non-Jewish bride (the other way around was not as frequent, nor certainly as important, though no more approved), the parents felt disgraced. In rigidly orthodox families, they would literally sit *shiva:* they would go into prolonged ceremonial mourning for the dead. Or, in less religious families, threaten suicide. All this was so clearly understood as being part of the "strangeness" of the Jews that even people who did not avow anti-Semitic views advanced this "clannishness' as one reason for their dislike.

The effect was nearly total endogamy. In 1920, Julius Drachsler published "Democracy and Assimilation," a study of 100,000 marriage licenses issued in New York City between 1908 and 1912. He found that of all white groups, the Jews were least likely to intermarry, averaging barely over one per cent. The Italians and Irish intermarried slightly more often. Significantly, the high-prestige-and-mobility nationalities, the English, Swedes, Germans, intermarried most often of all. Further studies in the thirties and forties confirmed the tendency on the part of Jews to marry each other. And that was that.

Or so it seemed. In time, the statistical composition of the Jewish group in America slowly shifted. Drachsler's statistics were heavily weighted toward those who came with the great waves of immigration toward the end of the nineteenth and the beginning of the twentieth century. These were strangers in a strange land, knowing nothing about it, and no one in it, except some fellow Jews who might have come earlier. The institution of the *landsman* was generated by the need, the solidarity, and the affection that people who had grown up in the same *Stetl* back in Europe had for each other in a new country. The newcomer

225

would look to the emigrant who had arrived earlier for help and advice. Is it any wonder that he often married his daughter or sister?

But things did not stay that way. As Jews moved into American society, the rate of intermarriage rose. Both the religious and the physical identity of the group became blurred. Thus the intermarriage rate among recent Jewish immigrants was 1.4 per cent, but the second generation had a 10.2 per cent intermarriage rate, and the third 17.9 per cent. If the trend continues, purely Jewish families are likely to be exceptional within one hundred years. (But, of course, that's "if.")

In comparative terms, the rate of intermarriage is still low; 21 per cent of Catholics intermarry. (Hardly the same thing though.) Yet the rate of Jewish intermarriages is rising. In 1957, the United States Bureau of Census found the average rate of intermarriage among Jews (all generations) had risen to 7.2 per cent.

By the nature of things, in a Gentile country, it is harder for a Jewish boy to meet a Jewish girl than a Gentile girl. On a random basis, on his job, at a party, at a beach, or in a bus station, well over 95 per cent of the girls he might meet are not Jewish. Unless he moves in largely Jewish circles, as many do, or lives in New York (which is the same), the Jewish boy—or girl—must actively desire to marry another Jew, or be precluded from marrying a Gentile, if intermarriage is to be avoided. For a Christian in America, almost any marriageable partner he casually meets will turn out to be a fellow Christian. Not so for a Jew. To be sure, Jews are concentrated in big cities where they can and do move in largely Jewish circles. But not that concentrated after all. The small-town Jew meets mainly Gentiles and a rising proportion of the contacts of even the big-town Jew are now with Gentiles—the more so the younger he is.

In Washington, D.C., 13.1 per cent of all marriages involving Jewish spouses were mixed marriages in 1956. But in Iowa, between 1953 and 1959, a minimum of 36.3 per cent and a maximum of 53.6 per cent of all marriages of Jews involved a Gentile spouse. There are few Jews in Iowa, and they are widely dispersed.

Most significantly, the active religious desire to marry only another Jew is slowly disappearing. The theme of Jewish boys marrying *shikses* begins to crop up in the books of Bernard Malamud, Saul Bellow, Herbert Gold, Philip Roth—Jewish writers, need it be said, who found the subject sympathetic or funny, or even sad. The writers were ahead of the sociologists.

Such plays as *Counselor at Law* or such movies as *The Jazz Singer,* both written and directed by Jews, in the past dealt with the ambitions of the Jewish newcomer to succeed in his new world largely dominated by established WASP families. How things have changed!

The Jewish hero, by means foul or fair, but largely because of his immense talent, succeeds. "Yet what is a man profited if he shall gain the whole world, and lose his own soul?" The Jewish hero endangers his soul by marrying— as a symbol of his success—one of those clean, cold, beautiful, and sterile *shikses*. But wait, fate—or is it Providence? —at any rate Hollywood, will teach him a lesson: a crisis occurs in his career. Everything he has achieved is endangered. Now, if he had married a nice, Jewish girl—like the adoring secretary in his office—she certainly would stand by him. But the *shiksa?* Well, what do you expect—she married him only because he was successful, and is perfectly willing to divorce him, now that he may fail. Even the children turn against him. What can you expect from goyish children after all? Did he have to send them to that expensive prep school where they learned to snub their father, let alone their grandparents?

Well, the crisis passes. And our hero never again will marry a *shiksa.* Mother knew best, after all. . . .

Thus the drama. It was, I believe, a true expression of how Hollywood—then, as now, largely Jewish—viewed the relation between Jews and Gentiles and repudiated its own temptation; perhaps the more true because the makers of these movies were not conscious of the views and values which they expressed, and which they had not always followed themselves. But that was first-generation Jewish Hollywood.

Today Hollywood would not say what it said then. The present movie-makers do not feel it. They still feel Jewish, but they no longer feel that the Gentile world is hostile and cold. Indeed, it has become remarkably hospitable, and they no longer feel that they are snubbed by it. Above all, they no longer feel that marrying a *shiksa* is a crime duly followed by the punishment of unhappiness and rejection in the hour of need. But this does not mean that marrying a *shiksa* has not remained also a symbol of success: on the average, Jewish men who do have significantly higher incomes than Jewish men who don't (of course, they are more emancipated as well).

Intermarriage is particularly frequent among the intellectual elite. Twenty per cent of the Jewish faculty members of the University of Illinois were married to Gentiles—and only 6.5 per cent of the Jewish townspeople. More piquant still, in New Haven 64 per cent of the Jewish psycho-analysts had Gentile spouses.* If one disregards the socio-logical facts (as psychoanalysts themselves do often enough) —the facts which relate the rate of intermarriage to income and status—one might wonder whether these analysts are all escaping their Jewish mothers. Or whether refugees from Jewish mothers are more drawn to psychoanalysis than others. (But your analyst might classify such reflections as resistance. He might be right, too: resistance and truth are not mutually exclusive.)

With the third generation of Jews arriving at marriage-able age in this country, the incidence of Jewish inter-marriage is soaring. Eighty per cent or more of the Jews in the United States today were born there—with a conse-quent vanishing of European, folk, or *Stetl* mores. In Wash-ington, D.C., intermarriage among these third-generation Jews has gone up to 17 per cent. It can be safely assumed that the rate in the rest of the country is keeping pace. To top it off, Jews—an educated, urban group as a whole —have only four-fifths the average birth rate of the rest of the population. In 1964 the ratio of Jews to the rest of the population in this country was 2.9 per cent. In the year 2000, it has been projected, it will go down to 1.6 per cent. And the few Jews remaining will not be very Jewish.

Fewer than half the children born of mixed marriages are raised as Jews, according to some statistics. Other sam-ples indicate that only 17.5 per cent of the children of

* Hollingshead and Redlich, *Social Class and Mental Illness,* New York: Wiley & Sons, 1958. New Haven may be too small to generalize—but the authors often do.

229

mixed marriages are identified as Jewish by their parents. Another estimate indicates that 70 per cent of these children are not brought up as Jews. According to rabbinical law, only children of a Jewish mother are considered as born Jewish. Most Jewish intermarriages involve Jewish men and Gentile women; their children, to be Jews according to Jewish law, would have to convert to Judaism unless their mother herself was converted.

In the past, anti-Semitism caused some Jews to see marriage to a well-connected *shiksa* as a quick step up the social ladder. August Belmont, the famous Jewish-born banker, is usually cited as the prime example. In *The Age of Innocence,* Edith Wharton described a fictional character, who, many people felt, was modeled after Belmont:

"The question was, who *was* Beaufort? He passed for an Englishman, was agreeable, handsome, ill-tempered, hospitable and witty. He had come to America with letters of recommendation from old Mrs. Manson Mingott's English son-in-law, the banker, and had speedily made himself an important position in the world of affairs, but his habits were dissipated, his tongue bitter, his antecedents were mysterious."

But when August Belmont married Caroline Slidell Perry, the beautiful daughter of Commodore Perry, all doubts were apparently stilled: he was asked if he cared to join the Union Club.

Anti-Semitism led other Jews to marry outside the faith for reasons which are allied to Belmont's but illustrate the reverse of the coin. That is, they did not wish to escape from Judaism to rise on the social scene, but rather to escape from the social scene entirely. They felt unwelcome, burdened by their Jewishness and by their position as outsiders and strangers. They wanted to sink into the comfortable obscurity of the majority.

"I'm not religious," said an advertising executive in Chicago, "so why should I pay the price of being Jewish? If I felt we were really the Chosen People, if I felt that God really had his eye on me—OK, who would care if certain country clubs wouldn't let you in? But I get no benefit from being Jewish; I only get the rough end of the stick for not being like other people. So I've stopped being Jewish. I married a Gentile girl, and we joined a Unitarian Church. I don't care much for it, but then I didn't care much for the Jewish synagogue either. So I leave it all to my wife. I never went to the synagogue, and I never go to church now either. But my wife has an answer when people ask what religion we are—and so do our kids. Why be a martyr?"

And for something you don't believe in? Herr Justizrat Marx, Karl's father, might have given a similar answer had he been asked. Not so his mother, who stuck to her Jewish background and was hated by her son.

Since many Jews have ceased to be religious, one might expect great numbers to wish to pass. But something holds them back. Few do pass. Even those who change their names still let their Jewishness peep through. They compromise with their ambivalence. To be Jewish—religious or not—is too much part of one's identity to be shed lightly or fully. And despite the defensive logic of the Chicago executive, most Jews would feel guilty, as though traitors, were they to deny their Jewishness—however doubtful its meaning has become to them. Thus, when the great French philosopher Henri Bergson returned to Judaism on his deathbed, after the Nazis invaded France, it was probably an expiatory gesture as well as a defiant declaration of solidarity. Yet if there is intermarriage, the Jewish identity can—and does—disappear in a natural way, not for the sake of disappearing, you understand, but after all the wife and children do have certain rights. . . .

These are what might be called the classic reasons for Jewish intermarriage—classic in the sense that they are mostly of a time that is past. With anti-Semitic bars almost entirely lowered in the United States, and especially in the urban (and urbane) circles that college-educated Jews tend to move in, other reasons for intermarriage are more frequently heard.

With the doors now open, many Jews are able to follow temptation. And what is more tempting than to escape once the locks have been broken? The famous closeness of Jewish families itself creates the desire. Once the outside pressure which prevented the escape from the family has gone, this desire may be indulged. And even the Jewish family does not always remain close enough to bar escape. Not for nothing do Jewish kids make up a disproportionately high number of the excitedly rebellious young. Pressure produces defiance—though often shifted to a symbolic parent. (The actual one is no longer there, or strong enough, to be defied.)

"I think the reason—or one of the reasons—Harold married me," says the Christian wife of a Jewish salesman, "is that he wanted a different kind of family life. I was attracted to the Jewish idea of a family. My parents were divorced, and I always thought the closeness of Jewish families in the suburb where I mostly grew up was a beautiful thing. You'd always see them together, and when they had a barbecue or something like that, many of the people there would be other members of the family. But

Harold called all that fetid and too close. 'They're suffo-
cating me,' he'd often say, 'I have to get away from Uncle
Lou and Aunt Helen and Sister Sarah.' He almost never
wants to go to any parties his family gives—Thanksgiving,
for instance, and I'm always fighting with him to go."

As for Harold himself: "You may not like this," he
says, "but I just did not want to marry a Jewish girl. The
Oedipus complex tells us that you're afraid of marrying
somebody like your mother. You may secretly want to, but
on the top level, the level of action, you're afraid of it. But
somehow you're not supposed to be aware of it. How could
you not be aware of it today? Every party you go to, everybody you meet is a psychoanalyst or patient or, most often,
a patient acting as though he were a psychoanalyst. I was
especially aware of all this, because it quickly came home
to me that the girls I liked were all the same: they were
thin, and most of all, cool. Not like the slang word, but in
the old-fashioned sense of having a little distance, a little
air around them. How long did it take me to figure out that
was the opposite of my mother? I love my mother, but I
didn't want to be suffocated once more in sour cream, or
drowned in chicken soup.

"The problem was, all the girls I met were Jewish.
Most of the people we know here in this suburb are Jewish.
All the people I work with are Jewish. But one of the other
salesmen in my company was a swinger. I began to go
around with him, and pretty soon I met a lot of non-Jewish
girls. And one of them I married."

Harold's mother: "I like Ann. I have nothing against
her. But in my heart of hearts, I can only feel Harold did
it to hurt me. Marry her—he did it to hurt me. I keep asking myself over and over, why did he do it? What did his

father and I—what did we do wrong? We gave him a fine home, a fine education, he always had nice friends. Now I have a daughter-in-law who I know makes my son very happy. So how can I be against her? But in my heart of hearts, how can I be close to her?"

Harold's father: "When I was Harold's age, I was a radical. I was for changing everything, freeing the oppressed, making it a better world. All right, Stalin and time changed all that. I never was for Zionism because I felt Zionism would be a step in the wrong direction. We had to make it all one big socialistic world—not just a bunch of little countries that were always fighting each other. Hitler changed all that for me: I give to Israel all I can. But deep in me, I still have this old feeling. That people should understand each other, work together, fight side by side, that no one should have the right to hurt anyone else, to say, 'You live here,' or 'You can only do that kind of work,' or, 'You're not good enough for me.' So when Harold came home and told us that he was going to marry a Christian girl, I was heartbroken. But how could I tell him not to? It would go against all my beliefs in the common humanity of the world."

When questioned further, Harold's father nevertheless said he wished Harold "could have found himself a Jewish girl to make him happy." When Harold was asked whether he wished his children to marry Jews or Gentiles, he replied that he didn't care.

On the other side, many Gentile girls today find an extra kick in the idea of marrying Jewish boys. Jewish boys are, on the whole, said to be steady and reliable and they don't drink. At least they drink less. They have a considerable reputation for earning money and for being good husbands and good fathers. And to all this good, solid, middle-class, family-raising virtue, they bring the current glamour of being, by definition, outside the conventional establishment. Like the thrills-without-danger appeal of a roller-coaster ride, marriage to a Jewish boy often seems heady indeed to a Christian girl—but also safe.

"Who does my father think he is," says one suburban Gentile girl who is married to a Jewish lawyer, "objecting to Lawrence? Lawrence is better educated than my father ever dreamed of being, he's politer, nicer to people—*and he doesn't drink.* Sometimes we go to parties at the club, and I know there are one or two people there like my father—older people, mostly—who think I made a mistake marrying a Jew. But by the end of the evening, when their husbands are falling all over the floor and I'm practically the only wife who does not have to drive her husband home, I know how smart I was to marry Lawrence. And I'll tell you something else that Lawrence himself would never mention: he makes a whole lot more money than my father, too."

The Jew seen as the symbol of rebelliousness takes on other forms that make him desirable to many Christian girls.

"Anti-Semitism," says one pretty delegate to a New Left convention, who is married to a Jewish boy, "is like old politics. It's irrelevant. People don't even bother to argue that 'it's a bad thing' any more. Save your breath. To have to argue in favor of the Jews today would be as useful as arguing in favor of water. Who's against it? Only irrelevant people, and they have to be attacked on more important grounds than that. You don't attack Johnson or Rusk because they have bad breath, but because they want to bomb and burn people. You can't waste time on the unimportant issues. You just ignore them.

"Harry helped me to see all this. I mean, you go to a good school, you get a good, *liberal* education—isn't that a laugh—and then you're supposed to forget it all, go back to the town in which you were born, raise a family, and go to church every Sunday. And then you're dead, and you never really lived at all.

"I just made a joke about the word 'liberal,' and usually it is a joke. But Harry was the first genuinely liberal boy I ever met. You always hear that about Jews, but perhaps I just hadn't met many Jews before Harry. At least, he was the first one I ever went out with, and talked to seriously.

"He seemed so different from the boys I grew up with. So interesting. You didn't have to wonder what Topics of Conversation Have We in Common? Harry was always on fire about this or that, and he could bring it to you, get you wrapped up and into it.

"I'm sort of idealistic—a holdover from when I was a religious little girl, I suppose. (No, today I have no religion at all.) And I always wanted an idealistic man. When Harry came along, I grabbed him. If only my mother could see me now."

These are the justifications. On a deeper, less conscious level there are perhaps more important causes for the attraction of Jews and Gentiles to each other, the attraction that strangers have for each other. The ultimate effects allow little doubt: if present trends continue, the Jews, having become part of America's financial and cultural establishment, also have begun to vanish.

236

17

Jews and the Promised Land

DURING the many centuries of the Diaspora, Jews all over the world included a fervent prayer as part of the rites of Passover. In no matter what language they said it, the promise to each other was always the same: "Next year in Jerusalem." For many Jews this prediction has now come true; for others it could be fulfilled should they actually so desire.

Many Jews went to Israel as soon as it became possible because they wanted to; others went because it became impossible to stay where they were—and Israel was the only alternative for them. This was the case of many who came from the Near East, and of others who fled Hitler in Europe. One of the reasons the late Israeli Prime Minister Levi Eshkol put pressure on the American Jews to emigrate to Israel, as Ben Gurion did before him, was that only the United States and Russia have any sizable Jewish communities left within their boundaries. The Russian Jews would like to, but cannot go: the government does not allow Jews, or other Russians, to leave the USSR. The American Jews could go but do not want to—though those who celebrate Passover may still include the ritual prayer in the proceedings: "Next year in Jerusalem." But not this year, and probably never. Why?

In the ten years before World War I, during the period of the first great Jewish immigration and settlement in what was then Palestine, only a bare handful of Jews went there from the United States. By 1948, when the State of Israel was established, there were under 10,000 American Jews out of a total population of 650,000 Jews. Today, the figure may be only 20,000 or 25,000. No wonder Mr. Eshkol and his predecessor, David Ben Gurion, were disturbed, however diplomatically. The American Jews will send their dollars—and they have been generous. Their hearts may be in Israel, but not the rest of their bodies. Yet the Israelis want Jews, body and soul, not just money. The American Jews are the most educated and skilled, and they are the most useful and needed ones. But they prefer to visit. The very dollars, which they send so freely to Israel, keep the American Jews in the United States. They are not only too prosperous, they are too happily settled down into that great middle estate, which is the ambition of the greater part of the human race, to want to rock the boat—or to take one.

Reluctance to emigrate to Israel is reinforced by unhappy experience. Those rare American Jews who do go to Israel and like it stay there and thus do not come back to propagandize. And when they write back, it is to brag about the hardship they are willing to endure. Those who go to Israel, and do not like it, do come back. They talk about the hardships they were unwilling to endure. Like lovers who somehow feel cheated by the beloved, they are very verbal about their disillusionment.

238

"The problem for an American who emigrates to Israel," said one such returnee, "is that he's got it in the back of his mind that he's leaving a culture in which he has been taught that he has inherited the world—even if he's a Jew, he's inherited it by virtue of being an American as well. Now he's coming to a country which, clearly more primitive, materially at least, than the country he left, nevertheless feels itself morally superior to his old country and therefore to him. He went to help them; they feel— and make him felt—that they are helping him. [Both are right, perhaps. But they don't feel comfortable with each other.]

"He wants Israel—his new country—to be better than his old one. After all, that is why he is leaving the United States. For a better place, he thinks. But he doesn't want his new fellow citizens to be or feel morally superior to him. But they do."

Americans in Israel are ever so slightly patronized as spoiled children, people who don't understand. They haven't been through the Nazi persecution, the liberation, the Arab wars. Neither their capacity to suffer nor their capacity to fight has been tested as that of the Israelis has been. They are just rich. Richer, indeed, than the sufferers and the heroes. Which somehow seems wrong. And more, the American Jew, poor fellow, doesn't even speak Hebrew, the language of Israel. And like most Americans, and unlike many Europeans, he doesn't have a knack for picking up languages quickly and easily. The result is that in the end he comes to feel that he traded the comforts, the ease, and *heimischness* of America for a less comfortable country where instead of being admired for his idealism in coming, he is looked down upon and treated—well, the way newcomers often are treated anywhere. But Americans find it particularly hard to be patronized. Above all, once they are abroad they discover how American they are. In America, they may feel that they are Jews. But in Israel, they feel they are Americans.

"The Americans who come to Israel," says an Israeli medical student at Columbia, "know that there is one thing more precious than anything in the world. Their blue-green American passport. No matter how fired up they are in the beginning about Israel, they always keep that ticket back home firmly in their pocket. They are very romantic about Israel, and so, naturally, there is a counter-emotion that soon sets in. A disillusionment. They begin to swing between the two worlds, traveling to and from, up and back. They come to Israel with stars in their eyes, but soon discover that Israeli pioneering is nothing like the technicolor movies of the American West which shaped their dreams. They then decide to go back to the United States. But once there, they begin to get fed up with the life there—the process which brought them to Israel to begin with. 'There is no idealism in America,' they tell us. 'You don't feel you're one of a people, building something together.' And in Israeli eyes, these are valid criticisms of the United States and its economic system.

"And so they make their second trip to Israel. Back and forth they go, an entire colony of people who all know each other, at home in both countries and really not at home in either. Maybe the problems with the American Jew is that, unlike almost any other Jew in the world, he is not forced to go to Israel, and if he does decide to go there to see for himself, again unlike all the other poor Jews in the world, he is not forced by economics to stay there. The American Jew can always buy himself a ticket to go back, and he has country which will take him back. It is this lack of commitment in the American Jew which makes him seem like a dilettante to us."

Nor does this would-be emigrant get much encouragement from his Jewish friends in the United States. "Maybe it's because they are all guilty themselves for not going," says one Jewish boy who has switched from studying medicine to agriculture to prepare himself for a life in Israel after graduation. "Whenever I tell my friends that I am going to live in Israel, they look skeptical or laugh at me for being an idealistic nut. When I told my mother, she looked as if I'd said I was going to marry a *shiksa*. 'But it's so far away,' she cried. 'And those Arabs, they're always making wars. It's dangerous there. Why don't you wait a few years, and then if you still feel like it, go. But right now?' But I don't want to be like those people, the only way you know they're Jews is that they eat lox and bagels, and go to Miami in the winter. If I'm a Jew, I want to be a Jew, and that means going to Israel."

An American who has lived in Israel for over a year and who is back to pay a visit to his parents, speaks of his difficulties in adjusting to life in Israel:

"It's like here in America, where there is a whole bunch of people who used to say, 'Don't say anything against [Joe] McCarthy. The guys will think we're all Communists.' Or, 'Jews shouldn't march in the civil rights parades, because the bigots will seize on them for the worst persecution.' In Israel, there is a whole party of Americans who always feel that the Israelis have their eyes on the Americans, waiting for them to do something 'American' and therefore foolish. And they're not entirely wrong. Jerusalem, for instance, most of the time, has a marvelous climate. But don't let the tourist posters fool you. It gets cold in the winter. And the Israelis—you ought to hear them bitch about it. One day, I was in someone's house—an Israeli couple I had gotten to know. They spoke English. I said something about the cold. And a French girl, Jewish, but French—she spoke English, too—turned to me with a terrible look of contempt. 'Well, of course all of us weren't raised with central heating,' she said. 'We poor peasants have had to grow up used to the cold.' I was stunned. After all, the Israelis themselves spend an awful lot of time complaining about the cold. But an American is not allowed to. Everybody there is so suspicious of Americans, so jealous, I suppose, of American affluence, that they are always looking for reasons to dislike us. For the past two thousand years, the world has been suspicious and angry at the Jews because they were supposed to be so rich. Now the Israelis feel the same way about the Americans.

"But if my Americanness separates me from the Israeli Jews, where am I? Who am I? But worse than that, this separation keeps me from making the final commitment, and giving up my American passport. And that is the very thing that will end this separation for all time. The very thing, but the only thing. It's like contemplating a marriage. You both want to and you don't, and you keep holding the girl's hand but delaying the ceremony."

An Israeli businessman speaks about why Americans are so often viewed with something less than admiration by

Israelis. "I think what I object to is their particularly American moral earnestness. They have a desire for renunciation, for assuming guilt, that I think is a blend of the worst aspects of both Jews and Americans. For instance, when the militant black nationalists in America make speeches saying, 'We hate Jews, give us money so we can buy guns to shoot our enemies,' the American Jews all applaud and raise funds, and Jewish lawyers fight to get these men out of jail.

"So the Americans come here—I'm not talking about the rich tourists who have not really come to Israel, I mean those Americans who are seriously thinking of emigrating. They come to Israel, and they want to fight the Arabs, they want to suffer in the desert. They cannot accept the relatively few, simple pleasures available to them here. And so when we tell them there is no war at the moment, that they are ill-equipped for the desert, they become hopeless and despondent and very often go back home right then and there.

"The rest, slowly, get used to it. Their money is usually running out after a while, so they have to. They get used to our diet—so different from the rich American diet. They get used to our inexpensive pleasures. Talking to friends. Going to a concert. They begin to feel they are really getting into Israeli life. After all, this is a kind of renunciation of American pleasures, isn't it? They think it's charming not to have hot water. They brag about learning how to repair a leaking kerosene stove. They are still playing at suffering, you see. They enjoy the picture of themselves doing without decadent American material pleasures.

"After a while, they go into their next stage, if they

stick it out long enough. They stop being American, and they stop thinking it charming to be cold or hungry or blistered by the desert. They get mad at it—like us. But we can do nothing about it, except stay mad at conditions and work to improve them. However, the American, when he suddenly realizes that this whole experience is not his Junior Year Abroad, that it is the rest of his life, and that the discomfort will never stop—he suddenly remembers he has another choice. And so he goes home. To the United States. Except those, of course, who can afford to move into luxury apartment buildings, and so on. Oh, Israelis who can afford to do so—they move into those places, too. Why not? But if you want to live in luxury apartments, with all that implies, why come to Israel to do it? You might as well stay in New York."

Here's another opinion on why Americans come to Israel. "They come because they want controls," says a tourist official. "They think they want to work for the common good, for a national purpose. But they don't. They want to be told what to do. You can't blame them. The United States is perhaps the most anarchistic country in the world. There is no social organization, no fraternity in the United States, merely peace treaties between various groups and individuals—treaties that are always breaking down because the people have a philosophy which tells them they have nothing really in common but this abstract idea of Americanism.

"And anarchy is the most frightening thing in the world. So Americans glamorize the *kibbutz* life: order, continuity, communality, and the cows must be milked seven days a week, no matter what. Above all, in my experience, the Americans glamorize the idea of no private property on a *kibbutz*. No people in the world have a better idea of the destructive power of private property than Americans."

Israeli statistics show that only a very small proportion of those who came from the United States work in the *kibbutzim*. Most Americans who go over tend to remain in their old professions. Doctors remain doctors, architects put up buildings, lawyers set up practice again as soon as they are licensed.

"They come on some dream," says the sabra who is studying medicine at Columbia. "They are not radicals who want a new society. They are not religious, not dedicated to the idea of Jewishness. They have come to bathe in the warm water bath of all they had heard about Israel when they were children. OK, so they didn't like American materialism. But how are they living here? After all, if you're going to pursue a career for the sake of pursuing a career, why not do it in the United States where there are more opportunities? And besides—where you already know the language?"

Many of the problems of American Jews in Israel begin with the language. Ironically, Israelis call all English-speakers *anglo-saxonim*. A Jewish friend of mine told me how he went to see some friends of friends who lived in Tel Aviv. The son of the house, a boy of about eight, was playing nearby, and he and his pal were introduced. The two boys had a conversation in Hebrew, obviously about my friend. When they had left, he asked what the boys had said. There was a moment's embarrassment, but he pressed for a translation. "Our little boy's friend asked are you a Jew, and our little boy said, 'No, he's one of the *anglo-saxonim.*' "

Throughout Israel, English is the second language, particularly among the government, university, and moneyed classes Americans are likely to meet. Therefore, the need to learn Hebrew is not overpowering. And it is an arduous job to learn not only a new language in which not one single root has a familiar ring, but a new alphabet as well. And why bother to learn the language if there is a sneaking suspicion that one might not stay in Israel after all? Needless to say, not learning the language and the consequent barrier this leaves untranscended go to reinforce the notion of going back to America. At least one speaks a common language with people there. Communities are built on communication.

"But what turned me off most of all," says one returnee, "was the situation between American Jewish parents and their Israeli-born children. I would see it again and again in my friends' houses. It is the principal reason for which I gave up my dream of Israel, no matter how lovely it seemed. The American parents spoke Hebrew, all right. But not well, and not easily. There is a tremendous drive on in Israel for Hebrew, and all children speak it as a matter of course. I remember when I was a child how embarrassed I was—let's face it—by the broken English my parents spoke. Do I want to raise my children to think of me as a greenhorn?"

The question of Israel—going, staying, returning—is deeper than all this, however. For American Jews, it boils down to whether they actually want to become Jews once more. Are they willing to define themselves as Jews exclusively—not any longer as Jewish Americans? It would mean giving up something known and comfortable for something unknown but certainly uncomfortable. German Jews hesitated to do so even as Hitler came to power and made no secret of his malevolence. Even the ancient Jews left Egypt only under extreme pressure. Jews have wandered all over the world, but never voluntarily. No wonder American Jews find it easier to chant "next year in Jerusalem"—better still to pay someone to chant it for them—than to go. They feel guilty, though. So they pay their debt—with money. They are generous; they are proud of Israel; no doubt they will do everything they can to help and defend it. But leave America?

Not only is there no pressure to make them leave, but America has become positively attractive to Jews who, in numbers far exceeding their proportion in the population, occupy the upper ranks of the class and status system. They are, on the average, better motivated and more intelligent than non-Jews, and, therefore, necessarily rise when there is no pressure to keep them down. Elsewhere this has been an ambivalent blessing; no people is likely, in the long run, to allow itself to be dominated by a group felt as alien. Thus the Jewish rise always produced counter-pressures. But it is not as likely to do so in America. On the one hand, American Jews are so assimilated that they are not felt as particularly alien. On the other, the American people are not a homogeneous group of tradition-bound natives likely to resent Jewish innovators who recently joined and seemed to take over. Jews are just one of many groups that make up a heterogeneous America—and they melt into it almost as much as other groups do. Hence, chances of anti-Jewish pressure are small—and so are, therefore, the incentives to migrate to Israel.

In Israel, American Jews would not be brighter than the rest of the population. Israel would mean lower status —status is relative, of course—and in a smaller society to boot. American Jews are by now accustomed to being Jews within a non-Jewish population—which is different from being Jews within a Jewish population. And in America Jews had to make no effort to be Jewish. The environment did that. Thus, when it comes to deciding, are you Jewish or American, American Jews answer resoundingly, "Jewish Americans"—Jews who feel as Jews in America and are so felt, but who do not feel Jewish enough to make their Jewishness a legal and political nationality, and to live in Israel. They are an American subspecies now: Jewish, but the habitat is America. And likely to remain so.

Epilogue

I HAVE tried to suggest throughout what makes the Jews so Jewish—what their essential characteristics are and how they came to acquire and preserve them. The characteristics which identified and unified Jews, despite world-wide dispersion, were at least in part reactions to the non-Jewish environment and to its unremitting and often hostile pressures. But not altogether. The character and fate of the Jews were already distinctive when they invaded Canaan, long before their defeat and expulsion from Palestine by the Romans. Judaism (and anti-Semitism) existed long before Christianity, and there was a distinctive Jewish character before Jews became the scapegoats of the Western world. Belief in one God, in there being no others, and belief in the moral requirements of this God and in their chosenness set Jews apart apart from the beginning of their recorded history, long before their rejection of Jesus made them outcasts.

Reentry in Israel certainly will not reduce endogenous Jewish characteristics which distinguished Jews independently of ghettoization. It will, however, cause the Jews to be shorn of those traits of their character—mythical or actual—which were acquired in reaction to living among alien and usually hostile populations. Often these characteristics have identified "Jewishness" in the eyes of Jews and non-Jews alike.

Thus, some visitors (including Arthur Koestler, as well as French and American sociologists) have already remarked that the Israelis do not seem very "Jewish": they are bereft of ghetto characteristics and of those acquired from living as a marginal group among an alien majority. The observation is true, and it is fraught with ambivalence: thank God we are no longer exceptional; we no longer have to bear the special burden of Jewishness. But also: my God, have we lost our special destiny? are we no longer the chosen people? with our special burdens and sorrows— and our ultimate salvation?

In most minds the special destiny which made for Jewishness was related to, if not identified with, the status of Jews in the Gentile world. Surprise, even shock, and certainly nostalgia are among the reactions to Israel that one must expect—as well as pride and relief. As a nation among nations, the Jews can be special only in the sense in which each nation is. They no longer are a special element within all nations, nor a universal leaven.

The Jews who have returned to Israel are not the Jews who were compelled to leave thousands of years ago; nor is the country the same. These Jews have not created, therefore, a Middle Eastern kingdom such as existed in Biblical times, nor one akin to those organized in the Arab world, nor a theocratic state. They have created a modern parliamentary democracy. They are on the way to industrialize the country. Israel, although in the Middle East, essentially is a Western country, sharing the values, the ideas, the social, economic, and the political systems prevalent in the West. Israel will differ from other countries in the same way in which Italy differs from Germany, or France from England. Which is enough for some, but disappointing to others. The Israeli Jews will remain Jews, but Jews who have shed many old characteristics and acquired new ones.

The two principal groups of Jews remaining in the Diaspora are in the Soviet Union and in the United States. Those in the Soviet Union are not allowed to leave, although many clearly would like to. Those in the United States could leave but do not want to. Chances are that Soviet Jews will continue to resist the governmental efforts to stamp out their culture, their life style, and their religion. They will, in all likelihood, succeed no less, and perhaps more, than other Soviet nationalities—despite major Soviet efforts directed toward destroying their identity and their religious beliefs. Jews have survived such attempts before, although with great losses and much suffering each time.

Unless present trends are reversed, chances are that Jews in the United States will assimilate themselves out of existence. This may happen through a combination of intermarriage, secularization, and social integration. Each of these elements reinforces the other. The reduced impact of religion necessarily reduces endogenous cohesion and identification, and the reduction of external pressure reduces the exogenous element that contributed so much to Jewish survival in the past. As Jewish children mingle more freely

251

with Gentile ones, as Jews are less and less restricted externally and find less and less reason in their religion to restrain them from integration with the non-Jewish world, that integration will spread. In the next few generations American Jews will become hard to distinguish from other Americans. They will also lose their own feeling of distinctiveness. This will not occur at the same pace throughout. And orthodox sects may well succeed in maintaining a separate Jewish life-style in America by insisting on segregating themselves, as some orthodox Protestant sects did. And some Jews will go to Israel. But for most American Jews, the trend is unmistakably toward disappearance as Jews.

That much about the trend. Prediction as distinguished from prophecy must always be based on the visible trends, as qualified by foreseeable counter-trends, or obstacles. Yet history in the past has not shown itself to be easily predictable. Often the one prediction that has been correct has been that predictions, however sensible, cannot be relied on—history abounds with unforeseen elements which, by definition, cannot be predicted and which can make nonsense of the most rational prediction. Who could have predicted Hitler in 1920—fifteen years before he started killing Jews? Who in 1930 did foresee what he would actually do? What the past teaches is that the future is all unknown. Who, therefore, would be presumptuous enough to predict the fate of the Jews from now on?